Praise for *Ask Like an Auctioneer*

"Every woman on the planet must read *Ask Like an Auctioneer*. Dia Bondi undoes centuries of conditioning that told us to stay small and aim low. Her approach is simple and remarkably successful. This book will change lives."

—Kat Gordon, CEO, The 3% Movement

"*Ask Like an Auctioneer* is the gateway to your biggest boldest dreams providing you with the tool set and perspective to get what you want. Excelling at asking is a skill set that changes lives—and that's exactly what the book delivers on. Dia breaks down the process of asking in the most actionable and effective ways I've ever seen, including addressing mindset blocks in a way that will have you never thinking the same again. Reading this book will not only have you ask in a way that will unlock dreams but embody a version of yourself you wish you had gotten a chance to meet sooner! This book is filled with countless light bulb moments and I'm so happy I can apply her hard-earned insights to all aspects of my own life."

—Gesche Haas, Founder & CEO, Dreamers & Doers

"Dia is a force who inspires the reader to take action with confidence through a matter-of-fact, bold, and energetic style of writing. *Ask Like an Auctioneer* is a fundamental shift in the psychology of how we think and manifest outcomes in order to design our best life. This book made me want to re-think, re-design, and get up and go for my next big thing."

—Rob Acker, CEO, Salesforce.org

"As the CEO of Latinas in Tech, I understand the challenges women face in negotiating their worth and bridging the gender pay gap. This empowering book equips women with the strategies and tools to take control of their negotiations, allowing them to secure the recognition and compensation they deserve. With its actionable advice and expert guidance, *Ask Like an Auctioneer* is a game-changer for women striving for equality in the workplace."

—Rocío Medina van Nierop, CEO, Latinas in Tech

"For so many of us who have conflated our intrinsic worth (and worthiness!) with how people assign us value, this book is a wicked wake-up call and invitation to rewrite our own estimations. *Ask Like an Auctioneer* is an elegant and powerful work that unlocks human potential to be more courageous about how we ask and get what we want in our professional and personal lives. Thanks to Dia for fabulously representing the voices of so many women from all walks of life, who share their fears, desires, and successes on their journeys that now coalesce into a movement for a more equitable society. "

—Dino Anderson, Chief Culture Officer, Articulate and Lecturer, Stanford Graduate School of Business

ASK
LIKE AN
AUCTIONEER

ASK
LIKE AN
AUCTIONEER

How to
Ask for More
and Get It

ÐIΔ BONÐI

Matt Holt Books
An Imprint of BenBella Books, Inc.
Dallas, TX

Matt Holt is an imprint of BenBella Books, Inc.
10440 N. Central Expressway
Suite 800
Dallas, TX 75231
benbellabooks.com
Send feedback to feedback@benbellabooks.com

BenBella and *Matt Holt* are federally registered trademarks.

Printed in the United States of America
10 9 8 7 6 5 4 3 2 1

Library of Congress Control Number: 2023016850
ISBN 9781637744123 (hardcover)
ISBN 9781637744130 (electronic)

Editing by Katie Dickman
Copyediting by Alyn Wallace
Proofreading by Christine Florie and W. Brock Foreman
Indexing by WordCo Indexing Services, Inc.
Text design and composition by Jordan Koluch
Interior illustrations by Yuko Maruyama
Cover design by Brigid Pearson
Printed by Lake Book Manufacturing

Special discounts for bulk sales are available.
Please contact bulkorders@benbellabooks.com

To my family.
To my son, Sean, daughter, Arlie, and husband, Christopher,
who, in the midst of so much complexity in life, just gave me space to write,
encouraged me to get the work done, and help me lead with who I am.
You are all gifts, every day.
I love you.

Contents

PART III: YOUR BIG ASK PLAN

Introduction

Remember those parties and get-togethers when you were a kid? The house parties for your favorite aunt. The sunny summer get-togethers. The family reunions. Maybe a weekly gathering of family and friends after chores or soccer practice or your karate lesson. Everyone would be there—cousins, friends of cousins, cousins who aren't really your cousins.

For me, these events were usually at my grandparents' house. And I loved them because they meant shucking corn, swimming, and guzzling a tangy punch my family made by mixing grape juice and lemonade. These parties meant hearing my grandmother yell at my grandfather in Italian, and, above all, they meant mischief, and they meant sheet cake. You know, that velvety single layer sheet cake with the slippery frosting? I wanted some and then I'd want some more. I always wanted more. And getting a second slice required cajoling the adults guarding the food table, whose peering eyes monitored the number of helpings each sticky set of little kid-cousin fingers attempted to grab.

As soon as one of us kids whispered, "Let's get another piece," it was on. We knew our mission and our goal.

Mission: more treats.

Goal: cake.

Maybe it wasn't cake for you, but surely you remember your favorite treat—the one you pined for from the beginning to the end of the party.

We were so good at it back then—all the planning and scheming. Crouched in a circle at the corner of the yard, we'd devise our strategy. We knew we'd stop at nothing. Once we picked the right moves to make, we'd go for it. We'd fan out, bobbing and weaving through the crowd with a laser focus on our target. We'd start with the most difficult hurdle: usually, Mom. She was most often in charge of enforcing the one-piece-each-you've-had enough-sugar rule.

"Can I have another piece of cake?" we'd ask enthusiastically. Instantly met with a no and an eye roll, we'd move on to our next tactic. We'd enroll another, less gatekeeper-y gatekeeper, someone like your joyful aunt who offered a better but still so-so chance of getting you more of what you wanted. Met with "it's OK with me if it's OK with your mom," we knew we'd been thwarted again. Regrouping back at base, your cousins and not-cousins would gather around to report on the status of the mission and goal. "We got nothin'." Until we saw what a great time Uncle Jim was having, and boom! Uncle Jim was feeling generous, he knew what we were after, and he was aligned with our undercover mission. Glancing side to side to check for the presence of the sugar regulator, he tipped his chin up and said, "Go, now!" We knew cake was only steps away, but when we arrived at the table . . . only crumbs were left.

DRATS!

But no, we had the ingenuity, resourcefulness, and commitment to our mission, and we'd see that now our goal must shift. A new target. We scanned the other desert tables, and nothing! *Cookies?* Gone. *Pie?* Only the gross kind. *Pass.* What now? We'd be stumped but undeterred. The goal was shifting, but our enthusiasm for our mission would not. Remember? Remember when we'd stop at nothing?

"Hey! I know where Grandma keeps a jar of Halloween candy just for keeps." Snap! So we'd run upstairs, and, just as we're making our way to the pantry, we'd encounter Grandma looking all blissed out on account of the great party she was hosting, with all her family around looking happy and sun-kissed. So, we swooped in: "Grandma, the cake is gone. And we only got a little piece. Could we please have a piece of the special candy you keep?"

With a side-eyed look of love, she'd reach up to the cabinet and hand us the jar. "Don't tell your mom," she'd wink. And that was that. Cake was a no-go. But candy? Mission accomplished. New goal attained.

When we were kids and had our eyes on a prize, we all had this ingenuity and cleverness that let us find a way to get it. The ability to sneak around the party or the reception or the afternoon at the park and notice where the possibilities were. And even when thwarted, we were prepared to take a "no" and go back to the drawing board with our pencils still sharp. We could circle back to home base and devise a new plan. For us, a "no" wasn't an existential threat; it was a speed bump. Yes, there were parties after which we went home crying in the backseat of the car empty-handed—no cake, no cookies, no pie, no candy. But overall, when faced with something we wanted, we could tap our tiny genius and find our way forward. We'd use asking as our success strategy, understanding our mission and being open to how it may unfold. It was even *fun*.

Over time we lose that ingenuity. Stakes get high. Rejection means more. And we lose touch with our inner mad scientist who is willing to experiment and test and see what happens, joyful when the beaker breaks, and surprised and delighted when something unexpected emerges. But it's precisely when stakes are high that you most need the ingenuity and curiosity and determination you had when you wanted cake and ended up with candy, still happy and proud you found a way. You had it then, you have it now, and you can use it here.

This book is for your tiny genius.

IT STARTED WITH A TONGUE TWISTER

There I was—a seasoned communications coach well-versed in corporate speak and hailing from the world of professional development—surrounded by a hundred cowboys. Me, in a sea of ten-gallon hats and big, shiny belt buckles. We stood together, facing the front of the poorly lit hotel ballroom, elbows at our sides and hands stretched out, alternating a gentle right-left bounce with our hands to the rhythm of our tongue twister warm-ups. In unison, we practiced our chants in a chorus of numbers, one after another. "Ten-ten twenty-twenty thirty-thirty" and "two and a half, five. Seven and a half, ten. Twelve and a half, fifteen." Together, those cowboys and I spent ten long days at auctioneering school learning the basics of selling everything from livestock to real estate to art to mysterious five-dollar box lots you'd see at a neighborhood garage sale.

I'm comfortable on stage. I've been speaking in front of audiences for years and have coached countless influential leaders in business, global sports, and entrepreneurship on how to speak powerfully as both a leadership tool and to advance their businesses. But on my final day at auctioneering school, when it was my turn to stand behind the podium and auction my very first item, my heart nearly pounded right out of my chest. Where should I start? How much would I get? What if no one bid? What if I asked for too much? Too little? How would I stay in control no matter what happened? With my auctioneering coach—an extremely tall, leathery, unsmiling, "let's ride" type of urban cowboy—by my side, I opened the bidding at two dollars. The item I was selling sold in less than a minute. And that single minute started a cascade of realizations that would forever and radically change the way I approach every critical ask in my life and work.

But before we dig into that and how you can apply my strategies to your own asks, you're probably wondering how the hell I ended up at auctioneering school in the first place.

DRAW FROM EVERYTHING

For the past twenty years, I have cultivated a career as a "communications catalyst" for some of the world's top CEOs, philanthropists, innovators, and creatives. Through workshops, speaking, and private coaching, I help leaders and entrepreneurs find the courage to speak from the heart and create the impact they want to have in their organizations and in the world. I help them speak powerfully so they can align people, teams, and cultures toward shared goals; get the votes they need; or close the deals that will change everything for themselves and their companies. At top companies across the globe and for the next generation of transformational start-ups, I teach my clients how to tap into their purpose and command the moment when stakes are high.

My work is nuanced, my approach is interdisciplinary, and my curiosity about our world is boundless. Over the years, I've sought skills and frameworks outside the discipline of communications, trusting that I could apply what I learned to my work. And if I didn't see a way to draw on the skills, frameworks, or new ideas I gathered, I still had a great time discovering and learning. I've taken workshops in applied improvisation and in the art of writing a spiritual will. I've attended workshops on open-source principles, design thinking, and the Thiagi Group's methods and games, and have participated in online courses on gamification. I learned to ride a motorcycle in my thirties, and discovered something called countersteering. I humiliated myself on stage in a one-woman show writing class in my early thirties and in my forties I picked up obstacle course racing.

Throughout all of these experiences, I'm constantly having a blast, while simultaneously pattern-seeking and pattern-matching, unearthing concepts to advance my clients' success and my own mastery in my career. I've used the idea of countersteering—the idea that while driving a motorcycle, if you want to go right, you lean right but push the steering toward the left—to allow my clients to take more control on stage. When they're struggling, we try something that's the opposite of what they're doing and voila! They're more in command when they're countersteering and it works even when doing so feels counterintuitive to them. And I've leveraged thinking prompts from the profound world of spiritual will-writing to get my clients to name and claim their impact, igniting their purpose and invigorating their leadership voice. There are lessons to be learned everywhere. They freshen my perspective and enable me to dislodge my clients from where they're stuck.

My wide-ranging adventures are part of my magic. Auctioneering school was no exception.

Approximately every seven years, I take a working sabbatical. One night, at the beginning of my last sabbatical, I was chatting with my husband about what I might do or learn during my time off and he reminded me of something I'd said many years before when I had been invited to be an MC and auctioneer at a small fundraiser. I'd never done it before and knew nothing about it at the time, but I bumbled my way through it and had a blast. Weeks later at a dinner party, I shared, "One day, I'd like to learn how to *really* be an auctioneer."

My husband suggested that maybe now, during my sabbatical, was the time to do it: to *really* learn how to be an auctioneer. Was it outside my discipline? Yes. Would it require entering a whole new world? Yes. Was it exciting? Yes. It felt right, so I registered for auctioneering school that same week.

Since then, I've taken my ten days of training and claimed auctioneering as an impact hobby: I offer my services as a fundraising auctioneer for women-led nonprofits and nonprofits benefiting women and girls. I've been honored to serve as auctioneer at fundraisers for fantastic organizations that are changing lives, lifting others up, and making an impact on social issues across categories including elevating economic viability for women and girls, tackling racism through media, health equity and health care, environmental stewardship and access to open space, and arts education.

Once I was deep into auctioneering, I realized that I wasn't just learning to get the best price for a VIP vacation or a massive piece of artwork, and I wasn't just learning to secure donations for the mission-driven organizations I represented at fundraising events. I was also learning how to courageously and strategically ask for more—and get it. I was learning to think in ways that encouraged me to ask for more. I was using a mental model that challenged what I thought was possible in a single ask, leveraging my auctioneering skills to ask for more each time there was an ask to make. Soon I knew how to approach an audience, set up an ask, and make it. I was able to drive donors toward a fundraising goal that meaningfully impacted the nonprofits I was supporting. And I was *loving* it.

Pretty soon, asking felt fun instead of scary. Asking became an experiment and a challenge that yielded surprising results. And then it hit me:

What if others could use these ideas and strategies to ask for more and get it? What if others could borrow from the world of auctioneering to unlock the potential of every ask and to get more of what they needed in order to reach their goals? What if we all asked like auctioneers?

And I knew where I could have the biggest impact because I knew who could use it most: women.

In my twenty years as a communications expert, I've noticed that the women I work with wring their hands about asking for more, whether it's for more money, more opportunity, more credit, or more exposure for themselves and their businesses. As a woman in business, I've struggled with this too. Even the smartest, most accomplished woman will ask for *what she thinks she can reasonably get* rather than asking for more and seeing what's possible. She's afraid that if she demands too much, she'll get nothing at all.

I've had very few conversations with men where they express hesitation around asking for a raise, a promotion, or a chunk of venture capital. Women, on the other hand, put pressure on themselves to make the perfect ask lest they fall to ruin and trash their professional reputations.

As the recipients of cultural messages like "If you put your head down and do the work, you'll be rewarded," and "Don't overstep your bounds," and "You don't want to look too ambitious," it's no wonder women worry about asking for what they want or need. And because of these mes-

> "
> *She's afraid that if she demands too much, she'll get nothing at all.*
> "

sages, we've been trained to believe that asking for something "acceptable" will guarantee a "yes." Historically, we are not the power holders or the power brokers. While burning on the inside, many of us have heard people tell us, "Well, it's not all about the money" and "You know, title isn't everything."

We get nervous to push our luck, thinking we might only get one chance at that raise, this client, that project, this job. Women secure less than 4 percent of the available venture capital, and are easily discouraged during the process of asking for the funding they desperately need to grow their bad-ass ventures. McKinsey's Women in the Workplace 2019 study showed that women ask for raises and promotions at an equal rate to men, but have their asks met less often. My women clients complain to me about the whispers they hear from their own inner voices—the ones telling them to give up, fall in line, and or just wait it out.

I tell them to silence those voices. There are a million asks women can make to a million different entities. And when we do ask, I want us to challenge what we think is possible and go big with enthusiasm, courage, conviction, and confidence. I want women to ask for more and get it. Because when women have resources and authority, things change for everyone. Studies show that when women have more resources, they put more of them back into their communities than men do. (Sorry, dudes. Facts.) You know the phrase "a rising tide lifts all boats"? When women have more decision-making power, boom! Up goes the tide. Women in executive roles are often sponsors of affinity groups or initiatives aimed to elevate and accelerate women's careers and impact. Women who run things, change things. Maybe you've seen or enabled a smaller example of this—and small is good too. One small change at a time has a big impact.

More decision-making power includes the ability to say no, walk away, and go out on our own when we realize that established systems aren't serving our best interests. In 2016, advertising icon Cindy Gallop gave the keynote address at the 3% Conference, and centered it around the idea of GTFO ("Get the Fuck Out."), a concept she still lauds to this day. Gallop insists that if you're working somewhere where your unique skills, talents, or perspectives are not valued, GTFO. GTFO and create something that gives you agency, something that enables you to decide what you do and what you create. Part of being a great auctioneer is leveraging the ask to see where you stand, including when it's time to GTFO. Asking is a great way to get very clear on who wants to be in conversation with you and who doesn't want what you're selling. It helps you read the room, understand the system, and move swiftly when that system fails you, *without* playing small, pulling punches, or handing over your power. The techniques and strategies of auctioneering don't just help women ask for what we want; they help us know when to walk away.

We need those techniques and strategies. We need to learn new ways to ask for and get the resources that will help us reach our goals—to fill our toolbox with the right tools for each job. For years, I've been helping women entrepreneurs and leaders speak powerfully. I see now it's time to use what I learned in auctioneering to help them *ask* powerfully. If I can show women how to think like an auctioneer, they can ask like an auctioneer. They can never leave any money or opportunity on the table again, ever, ultimately gaining the resources and decision-making power needed to implement the changes that matter for themselves as well as their organizations and communities. This book is not an auctioneering school for girls. It draws on what I learned auctioneering in front of audiences large and small to help you advance yourself wherever you need advancing—and where asking can help you do it.

A few weeks after I first had the idea of teaching women to ask like auctioneers, I had the opportunity to test the appeal and applicability of my advice. I was invited to speak at a women's conference in Silicon Valley, and, in front of a crowd of sixty professional women, I shared how to ask like an auctioneer. When I finished my twenty-minute presentation, jaws were on the floor. The whole room said, "Holy shit! Keep going! We want more!" So, I gave them more. In 2019, I launched Project: Ask Like an Auctioneer to help one million women ask for more and get it. I launched it as a keynote and workshop teaching thousands of women how to ask for more and get it—so they can courageously and confidently reach their goals—using the mental models, ideas, and strategies I took away from my adventures in the world of auctioneering.

Since launching the project, I've brought these ideas to women's initiatives at the world's premier technology companies, to women's professional associations for groups including real estate professionals and entrepreneurs in social impact, and to organizations that support women of color in international peace policy and for professional development communities and employee resource groups focusing on early and midcareer professionals in tech. The women in these audiences have told me stories of the critical asks they make every day—asks that elevate the visibility of their work or drive their financial security and wealth. They ask for promotions, angel investments, and support for their emerging endeavors. They make fundraising asks that support women running for office at local, state, and national levels. These asks are critical to the success, advancement, and resourcing of their goals and dreams.

Whatever the ask, it's time for more women to have the chance to learn how to ask like auctioneers.

YOU CAN ASK FOR MORE AND GET IT

This book is an idea-packed, actionable guide engineered to support your desire to ask for even more and then go out and get it. The chapters build on what I've already shared with audiences across the country, offering fun and practical lessons alongside anecdotes from real women who've learned to ask like an auctioneer. You're going to rip through this book and get "do now" ideas and strategies you can put into action even before you reach the final page. In the pages ahead you'll find:

- The one idea that can maximize the potential of every ask
- Nine ideas from the world of auctioneering that can be used in a business context to help us ask for more and get it
- Eye-opening anecdotes and examples from my twenty years of coaching, as well as from the auctioneering stage, that illustrate the success of these strategies in real-world contexts
- Stories about and from real women who've used these strategies to either get exactly what they want or at least gain critical knowledge by asking
- A plan for building a powerful ask if you don't already have one

Auctioneering school was a lot like driving school. You learn what numbers to use, scripts for opening and closing bids, and the simple technique of raising the bid amounts. You stand in front of the class and practice your numbers and get a feel for when to sell whatever lot you're selling. Taking turns for a solid week, I'd hear: "Well dagnabbit, Dia, if nobody else is biddin' then sell the gosh darn thing. Just say sold and get on with it. And don't forget to say their paddle number. Next!"

After I grasped those basics, I took my new skills out on the road, where the real learning started. Over time, standing in front of audiences, calling numbers, and shouting "Sold!" I started to notice what worked well when I made an ask and how I could better set myself up for success. I found that some of the basic best practices I learned in auctioneering school did more work than advertised, helping me to supercharge my asking. Over a few years of practicing auctioneering, I honed the principles you'll learn in this book into ideas and strategies we can all use when we ask for what matters. The ideas and strategies I present are so simple, powerful, and actionable that as soon as you understand them, there'll be no going back.

In some chapters, you'll find journaling and reflection prompts. These are designed to help you integrate the ideas and lessons into your own life so they don't stay trapped inside this text. In that transition from the ideas living on these pages to them living with you, they'll morph and take new form, mixing with your lived experiences to create insights even I can't fully anticipate. Good. My hope is for you to take what I offer here and twist it into a shape that best fits the landscape of your life and goals.

Anonymized and retold here, every story I share connects to the woman who shared it with me—women who are in my Rolodex or who tapped me on the shoulder after a workshop or speaking engagement. In the years since launching Project: Ask Like an Auctioneer, through talks, webinars, workshops, and coaching circles, I've had the chance to hear and collect stories from women across industries, disciplines, life stages, and identities. Many of them have identities that are intersectional, bicultural, and multilingual. They straddle many worlds and live in the friction between them. Like my wish for you, they've taken these ideas and brought them into the context of their own lives and dreams. They've wrestled with the biases they face, tapped their ingenuity, and taken parts of what you'll learn here to make it their own, unlock the potential of their network, and unblock the path to their goals. I have a lot of gratitude for these women who raised their hands, asked their questions, and shared their stories.

I hope this book will inspire you to do things like:

- Get the biggest raise of your life.
- Gain access to the networks that matter to your goals.
- Position yourself for promotion and level up at your company.
- Secure the business partnerships of your dreams.
- Gain the visibility you need to promote your work or business.
- Negotiate severances that honor your work.
- Unstick what's stuck in your career or business.
- Fundraise with more confidence, whether you're launching a start-up endeavor, running for public office, or kickstarting that nonprofit you've always dreamed of running.

DO NOT USE AS DIRECTED

Your experiences and context are your own. We don't walk the earth facing the same challenges and biases or carrying the same privileges. In this book, I'll lay out ideas I've learned from the auctioneering stage, but they work better—maybe even work *best*—when you take into consideration your individual experience. Use the ideas here in a way that is sensitive to your context and the biases you face. Women with myriad identities confront bias inside and outside the workplace when negotiating and advocating for themselves. If you are a woman returning to work after raising children or caring for an ill parent; or are facing ageism; or are a woman with a disability; or are someone with a racial, cultural, gender, or sexual identity encountering biases that impact your experiences and the outcomes of your asks and negotiations, use the ideas in this book not as directed, but as needed. Similarly, if you are not a woman and reading this because it's time for you to ask for more and get it in your life, career, or business, take stock of your own unique situation. Consider your own context, your own life, and your own lived experiences. Because you know best!

And, most importantly, you don't have to do it alone. One of the most wonderful things about starting this project has been spending hours and hours with small, medium, and large groups of women who adapt these ideas to their own needs and, in doing so, offer invaluable help and wisdom to others in the group. As you customize these ideas to your career, goals, and life, trust your own wisdom and ask for collaboration with those you trust. I offer these ideas with enthusiasm—certain that they work—but I believe that the way you'll make them work best is by making them work for *you*.

So use as needed, not as directed.

IT'S NOT ABOUT NEGOTIATION

Ask Like an Auctioneer is not a book about negotiation. It is not a book about "manifesting" or "ask and thou shalt receive." Asking is not simply stating a desire and having the world provide. While we'll talk about mindset (kinda), this book is about taking action. It's about pragmatic, concrete strategic asking and some down-to-earth tactics for helping you do that and have a blast along the way. This is about running your shit like the CEO of your own life, career, and . . . well, business.

It's also a book about the sneaky ways we self-sabotage and lowball ourselves when we make pivotal asks, and how to overcome these pitfalls. It's a book about setting boundaries and honoring the voice on the other side of the table without silencing our own. It's a book about raising the stakes on every ask, while simultaneously lowering them enough that we can keep moving forward no matter what answer we get. It's a book about embracing our inherent worthiness. And, very simply, *Ask Like an Auctioneer* is a book full of courage-bolstering ideas and strategies that will help you take the actions necessary to ask for what you need to reach your goals in business and in life.

LET'S GO

We're going to go on this little journey, you and I, and here's how we'll do it:

Part one is all about how to ask like an auctioneer. Complete with a visual model, you'll be introduced to the idea that flips the script on the logic we use when we make an ask, and you'll learn about a little thing called the Zone of Freaking Out (it sounds way scarier than it is, pinky promise). It even has its own acronym! I bet you can guess what it is. In this part, you'll learn a new way of asking for more—an approach that once you see, you just can't unsee.

In part two, you'll learn the nine key strategies to help you ask like an auctioneer. Just because you know *how* to ask, doesn't mean you don't need a boost in order to do it. While the strategies are simple, they're not easy, but I'll bet at least one of the nine ideas will immediately help you kickstart asking for more, even just for a little more.

In part three, you'll get a six-step ask plan, so when you're like, "OK, I love this! But, what do I ask for?" you'll have a way to answer. In this part, we'll also grapple with some of the most common questions I've received from folks just like you. And I'll share a few frameworks for storytelling so when you have your ask plan in hand, you can actually say what you need to say to get that ask right out of your mouth or into an email.

Now let's go, go get it, and go start something here.

PART I

How to Ask for More and Get It

CHAPTER 1

You Will Be Too Much for Some People. Those Are Not Your People.

Y ou've got all you need to apply the ideas and strategies you'll learn in this book. You're well equipped with the smarts, the talent, and the self-awareness you need to develop your own schematics, run the numbers, and do what's right for you. You don't have to have all the answers, but I trust you'll find them if you're up for asking the kinds of questions that let you develop the answer that's right for you. Questions like, "What *are* my goals?" and "What *do* I want?" and "How do I want to go about getting it?" This book is all about what's right for you. And I'm not asking you to change. I'm offering you ideas and strategies you can use exactly as you are today. And you're gonna do it on your own terms. So we gotta get a few things straight. Read on.

REMEMBER WHO YOU ARE

Before we get going, let's adopt the stance we want to take as we move through this book together. What I love about this stance I'm about to share is that it makes space. It makes space for you to be who you truly are as you pursue the goals and dreams you have for yourself. It reminds us that we don't always have to carve ourselves down or shape ourselves up to get what we need to move forward. It creates space for you to recognize that who we are, what we want, and how we pursue what matters to us is not a liability; it's just that sometimes those things are mismatched to the situations we find ourselves in. In these scenarios, who you are, what you want, and the audience you're talking to or trying to collaborate with have the wrong kind of friction—it's not *you*, it's just that it's not right. This stance gives you permission to see misalignment and not internalize it, and instead use that recognition to step away from what's not working for you and toward what is. Here goes:

> *You will be too much for some people.*
> *Those are not your people.*

We'll use this idea throughout the book to remember who we are and hold on to that.

At the time I'm writing this book, I am forty-eight years old, and I am who I am. I get reminded regularly that I am intense. Maybe even too intense. Maybe you've heard it too. You're too loud, optimistic, enthusiastic, quiet, introverted, extroverted, energetic, demanding, slow, fast, analytical, direct, blah, blah, and the list goes on.

The thing is, what some see as a liability in you, others see as a strength to be admired. In this book, you are not a problem, and I'm not here to change you. You're perfectly imperfect and there's nothing about you I'm here to edit, audit, alter, or altogether transform. You are not a problem. I'm going to show you some ideas and strategies you can use, just as you are, to ask for more and get it so that you can reach your goals faster. On your path to do just that, you are going to get initial rejections, unsolicited criticism and comments, sour faces, ghosting, questions, and some flat-out noes that don't leave any room for negotiation. These responses are not invitations to change who you are or to give up on

"
Do you.
"

your dream for yourself no matter how big or small that dream is; they are moments to anchor yourself in this stance and keep going. You'll make adjustments and try new strategies and tactics, but fundamentally? Do you.

IT'S NOT JUST ABOUT YOU

SexTech entrepreneur and status-quo-challenging ad industry badass Cindy Gallop (yeah, her again) says when women "unashamedly set out to make an absolute, goddamn, fucking shit ton of money, [. . .] we need it to fund and help other women; help other women."

This quote is so powerful and at the heart of the why of this book. "Ask for more and get it" isn't about greed or amassing wealth, power, and resources for their own sake. I mean, if you're asking for more money and getting it so you can buy yourself that Lambo, OK, no judgment. But that's not the spirit of this work. I want to be a part of your journey to equip yourself with what you need because I know that when women gain more resources and decision-making power, it can change things for all of us. So while this book is about you, it's not *just* about you. You'll hear stories in this book of how women have used the ideas here to put themselves in positions that make it possible for other women and girls to see what's possible. Women have used the ideas in this book to gain status and promotion in their organizations, ask for money and sponsorship when they're running for office, and secure better salaries that have an impact on their own lives and the lives of the people in their households. Women have used these ideas to gain access to the networks they need to advance their goals and to own decisions in their organizations that affect hundreds of people. And their paths to achieving these things all required asking for more.

So yes, I want you to ask for more and get it, unashamedly, because when you get what you want, you have an impact on us all.

Sometimes the impact is direct. A woman gets a raise, now she's got more cash to activate in her philanthropy. An expert secures that big project that affords her to do more formal mentoring for a start-up accelerator supporting women founders. Your auntie asks big and now she is a decision maker on recruiting policies in a field in which women and underrepresented folks are implicitly filtered out or blocked.

Sometimes the impact is more indirect. Your sister asked big and secured a sabbatical that allowed her to sail through the Bermuda Triangle and vlog about it, sharing her story with millions of girls who, for the first time, see a woman solo sailing mystical waters. Inspiring even one girl to say yes to joining a summer sailing class would be a big impact.

Or maybe just the sheer act of advocating for ourselves in a very concrete way rubs off on others, such as in the case of one mom who, by asking for more and getting it in her own life and ascending, in a short time, from a low-level role in tech organization to director level, with the compensation that goes with it, flipped a switch in her daughter's brain. Her daughter was watching and learning, and while engaging in a digital creator platform, this twelve-year-old asked for a price for her art that got her a *no* on the token exchange, but gained her a status in her creator community that had a bigger upside than that single deal was worth to her. She asked like an auctioneer, because her mom had asked like an auctioneer. This shit rubs off. Over her lifetime, she'll take that skill, the skill she learned secondhand from the ideas in this book, and take control in her own asks, getting more of what she needs to reach her goals. It may be one ask here, and another there, but over time, those little moments will take her far. Small shifts now equal big gains over time. Her mom asked for more and got it, and *that* has the power to change everything for her daughter—for her household that, in her world, *is* "all of us."

ULTIMATELY, ALL YOU HAVE TO DO IS BE YOU

I've said that I hope this book helps you get more so we can make change. But I'm not asking you to do anything in particular. All you have to do is move toward your goals and, simply by doing that, you will cause change.

More women at the top (of whatever)? Change. More women making more plata? Change. More women doing what they do best and doing it well-resourced? Change.

Later you'll hear about Lorella the Brave. She used the ideas in this book to make moves, and, as she got into a decision-making position at work, all she had to do was be herself, every day. Just the simple fact that *she* is in the chair making decisions about recruiting, changes recruiting.

There's a lot of work left to do to continue elevating women and girls—giving them the resources they need while changing the systems we operate in that maintain the status quo—and it's tiring. And I'm not interested in piling on. You've got houses to run, kids to raise, aging parents to care for, recycling to sort. You've got climate change to consider, gun violence in schools to address. You have enough homework and enough activism to engage with. So when I say I want this book to help put more money and decision-making power in the hands of more women so we can make change, I'm saying we can do so by simply getting where we want to go, and being ourselves. It'll rub off.

FEEL LIKE YOU HAVE TO PUKE? THAT'S OK.

In Jen Sincero's book *You Are a Badass at Making Money*, she says when you go to get into action on your money goals, "Make sure it's something scary, something that you'd really rather not do because it's super uncomfy, something that makes you feel like you might puke." Yes, like you have to puke. The thing is, we too often read that feeling in our guts when we step outside of what we think is possible for us as a bad sign. A sign we're doing something naughty, and that we are about to get in trouble because "how dare you."

That feeling may never go away. That's fine. That feeling is telling you something important. It may be telling you that something matters to you, or that you care a lot about the outcome. It may be telling you that you're doing something courageous or that you're taking a healthy risk and challenging your assumptions about what's possible. And what it takes to trigger that feeling is going to grow with you. What feels big today may feel small in just a few weeks, months, or years, and you'll wonder, "What was I freaking out about?"

My daughter was scared the first time she walked up to a cashier with two bucks in her hand to buy a pack of gum. She felt over her skis and like she didn't belong, like she was doing it wrong. In second grade, she mustered the courage to ask her teacher if she could sit in the back of the room alone during reading time so she could concentrate better, and when she made that ask, she had that feeling—that feeling of "How dare I?" In sixth grade, her teacher told me she was a great student, really good at asking questions and getting clarity so she can do good work. All good things. And it sounds like she's more confident now, and she is. But she still gets that "pukey" feel-

> **"The asks you make will evolve with your growth and with your dreams."**

ing when she has to make a big ask. It's just that now, what causes that feeling is something bigger. It hasn't gone away, just changed as she's changed. As she's leveled up, what gives her that feeling of "How dare I?" has grown with her. Yours have too. It never goes away; it just moves with us.

Remember the first time you asked for a raise, or to play a certain position on a team in your favorite sport? Or, remember the first time you asked to sit somewhere specific on the bus, or made a request to be paired up with your best friend for a school project? What feels small today used to feel big to you. And that will just keep happening. The asks you make will evolve with your growth and with your dreams. As you level up, there will always be new levels up ahead. And that feeling of "How dare I?" may follow you. I talk to hundreds of women in my Ask Like an Auctioneer keynotes and workshops and everyone has their "oh shit" zone—at every stage in their professions and lives, from early career to executive level.

By the end of this book, I hope you'll reread that "How dare I?" feeling as a sign you're doing something courageous. That you're standing up for your dream for yourself and that you are being a champion for your goals. That you'll have a relationship with that feeling that is positive (and even a little fun!) because it's signaling that you are doing something you can be proud of.

And if you feel like you have to puke, it's OK.

MONEY IS A METAPHOR

When auctioneering, we're selling to the highest bidder and taking direct pledges in a fundraiser. In these situations, it's all about the money. In this book, I'll be talking about and using money-centric examples a lot. But money is a metaphor—it represents all the asks you'll make where you want to maximize the potential of that ask.

When the idea of Ask Like an Auctioneer first hit me, I assumed it would only apply to the money asks women will make—for compensation, investment, freelance rates, and the like. But no. Other things happened.

The year I launched Ask Like an Auctioneer, it was simply a talk I gave— and I was telling *everyone* in my network about it. That first year, I was doing our school's live auction for the annual fundraiser, and one of the parents and I struck up a conversation. I shared with him this wild project I'd launched called Ask Like an Auctioneer, and within twenty-four hours, he'd introduced me to the engineering director at a well-known streaming platform to suggest that my Ask Like an Auctioneer keynote might be a great fit for the Women in Technology summit she was organizing. I'll call this director Moira the Muse, as she is an engineering leader who marries the arts and sciences with absolute elegance. I went for tea with her to discuss how my keynote might fit into the programming for the event and she slapped me right upside my head (metaphorically, and gently but firmly). Moira the Muse loved the ideas in Ask Like an Auctioneer and invited me to speak at her summit. I blinked a few times and said, "Moira, thank you for the invitation, but I'm not sure this is a great fit. I really am talking about money and investment and targeting women freelancers, independent professionals, and founders."

Moira the Muse peered at me and said, "If you don't recognize all the asks we have to make on our path to fulfilling our professional potential, you're missing it. Plus, pay gap!"

She was right.

Yes, we'll talk about money in this book, but take what you learn here and apply it to every strategic ask you'll make—for money and for so many other things. Money asks are just one type of ask you'll make. After talking with hundreds of women, it turns out that there are four categories of asking and each of those ask categories can be a strategic move to accelerate you toward your goals. In later chapters, I'll share those four categories. Because auctioneering specifically deals with money asks, we'll be using lots of money examples. But those money scenarios function as metaphors for whatever ask you may craft in your life and profession. So don't get stuck on just the dollar bills—draw on all the lessons and use them where it matters most you to.

So, money is a metaphor to be applied as needed to ask for what you want. And, yes, you will be too much for some people. Those are not your people. Onward.

> *You will be too much for some people. Those are not your people.*

CHAPTER 2

How to Ask Like an Auctioneer

A fter a year or so of auctioneering for fundraisers, I got the hang of it. I was good enough at tracking my numbers, using the mic, and weaving together the narrative of the organization I was there to fundraise for with the sales of the items that were up for auction. I was getting my sea legs on the stage, growing into and finding my voice in the role. My concerns were shifting from keeping track of my numbers to being aware of what was going on in the room. The experience went from being really challenging, technically, to being a little fun, because I was becoming both competent and confident, which allowed me to not just do the auctioneering, but start to observe how it worked. And that's when it hit me.

My two worlds—leadership communications and auctioneering—collided. In one of the loudest aha! moments of my life, I felt like I'd been shocked into seeing something I couldn't unsee: *If all the women I work with and support could have the chance to do this wild thing—to stand on stage and see what it feels like to unabashedly ask an audience for something . . . if they were all supported by a scaffolding of ideas for how to successfully auctioneer an item, ideas for how to get the best price and not apologize for it, what would that give them? What would it do for women at every level, at every critical moment in their lives, careers, and businesses, to be able to ask like an auctioneer and know they've maximized the potential of every ask?*

I wasn't going to start an auctioneering school for girls, but that aha! moment planted the seed that grew into this book.

ASK LIKE AN AUCTIONEER

As a communications coach, my private clients and my skills-training participants come to me to strengthen their voices as leaders. And part of that work entails finding upcoming communications moments to workshop just that. We always start with understanding what they want from their audience. Then we build a killer communications strategy, presentation, or speech around that.

The question of "What do you want?" has two parts. First, "What is it that you want?" The answer is often things like budget, headcount, votes, time, attention, investment, or participation. Once I get that answer, I have to ask the next part: "How much of that thing do you want?" How much of your audience's money, time, or attention is necessary to reach the goal your presentation, pitch, or story is designed to support?

The answer to the question of "How much?" is often met not with a solid answer, but with a bunch of hand-wringing, head-scratching, and brow furrowing. Not because they don't have an answer, but because they're arguing with themselves about choosing the *right* answer.

Once they've gone around the block and back in their thinking, the response I most often receive to my question is another question: "Well, Dia, what do you think I can get?" And in the years before I learned to auctioneer, this seemed like a *great question*! I would conspire with my clients to design an ask, to decide "How much?" based on what we thought we could get. Need ten new engineers for your project, but think they'll only go for six? Great, ask for six and cobble together the rest of the team or learn to live without those extra hands. Need $120,000 for that campaign, but think they'll balk and only give you $80,000? Great. Let's ask for $80,000. And when we get a yes to those lower numbers, we'll feel great because we got a yes!

That's the problem—asking for, and getting, less because we're asking to get a yes. And I never saw it until I started to auctioneer! We shape our asks around what we think is feasible, rather than pushing the boundaries of what is possible. We shy away from anything that could get a no, and by doing so leave money and resources on the table.

Auctioneers don't do that. We can't! We ask *to* get a "no." We *must* ask in order to see what the maximum possible amount is that anyone in that room, at that moment, would pay. We need to ask for the *most* so we can get a "no" and are certain we've hit the ceiling and left nothing on the table. Then and only then can we say, "Sold!"

No is a good thing! *No* is great news! *No* is exactly what we're looking for because it tells us we've maximized the potential of that ask.

And, "no" is not the end. Once we get a "no," we sell the item to the person who will say "yes" to the price *just below* the price that got a *no* from the room. And voilà! We've found the price that is exactly at the equilibrium of what my audience will say "yes" to and the ask's maximum potential.

> " No *is exactly what we're looking for because it tells us we've maximized the potential of that ask.* "

That's what it means to ask like an auctioneer. Aim for a "no," and when you get it, jump for joy because that's when you know you've made the top ask, leaving no money or opportunity on the table, and that you're closer to getting what you can without selling yourself short. *That's* what deserves a pat on the back.

WELCOME TO THE ZOFO

Think of making an ask like this:

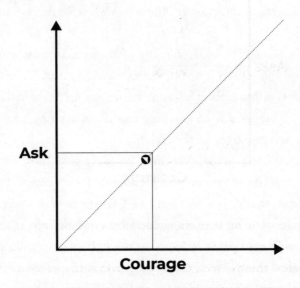

On the vertical axis, we have an ask. The higher up you go, the bigger the ask. On the horizontal axis, we have courage. The farther out you go, the more courage you're using.

There is a relationship between asking and courage—the bigger the ask, the more courage you need. For the sake of clarity and simplicity, let's say that the size of the ask is equal to the amount of courage we need to make it. It's one to one. Need to make an ask that's about three units in size? That'll require three units of courage. Looking at it on the flipside, the ask is limited by how much courage we can muster.

How much courage *can* we muster? About as much as we need to make an ask that feels kinda big, but still mostly guarantees a yes:

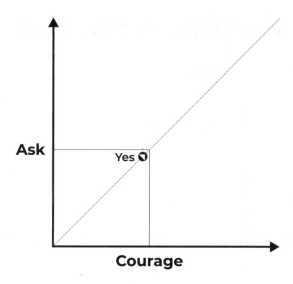

I'd estimate that most of us need to be somewhere between 85–100 percent sure we'll get a yes in order to make a particular ask. Because everything at or below that yes feels pretty cozy, safe, and like something we can bet on. In that way, the *yes* holds us hostage and dictates the size of the ask.

But what about all those increments above that mostly guaranteed yes, where other possible yeses could exist? Why don't we ask for those? Because those asks live in a place I like to call the Zone of Freaking Out—the ZOFO.

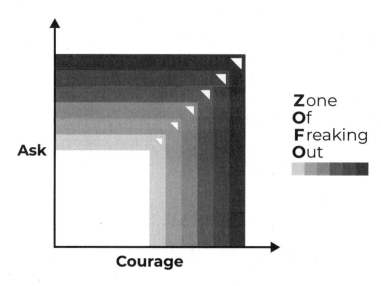

You know that feeling, right? That tingly, freaky, alive, *How dare I? Who do I think I am?*, *Wow, am I really doing this?* feeling. That feeling shows up when you're in the ZOFO, a space that is full of life, potential, and opportunity.

It's true—out there, at the farthest reaches of the ZOFO, lies a *no!* It's there. And it's not bad news if you get it. If you ask in the ZOFO, get a no, and negotiate down a click or a few clicks, you are likely to end up with more than if you'd asked in order to get a guaranteed yes. This is exactly what we do as auctioneers. And I want you to ask like an auctioneer every time you go to make a strategic ask that matters big-time to your goals.

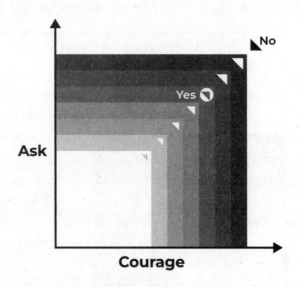

> **The ZOFO is the place where we stand up for our dreams for ourselves.**

We too often read the feelings we have when we're in the ZOFO to mean we're in a danger zone. What we don't realize, however, is that when we step into the ZOFO, we are opening ourselves up to growth and tapping into our greatest potential and the potential of that ask. The ZOFO is the place where we stand up for our dreams for ourselves. It's the place where we experience what's possible for us, and, like I mentioned in the introduction, my hope is that by the end of this book, you'll reread the ZOFO feeling as a sign you're doing something courageous. In later chapters I'll share stories of women who have stepped into their own ZOFO to change their lives and permanently alter the way they interact with rejection in negotiation. These women have used the strategies in this book to ask for more, transforming and accelerating the journey to their goals one ask at a time, on their own terms.

So hold on to the image of the ZOFO. The rest of this book is dedicated to helping you step into your own personal ZOFO, so you can challenge what you think is possible, go for no, and ask for more and get it.

#ZOFO

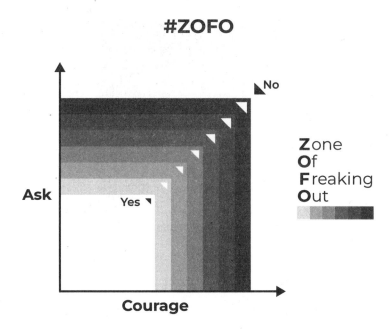

CHAPTER 3

The Ask That Changes Everything

When I was twenty-six years old, I made one ask that changed everything.

This single ask let me live my values, travel the world, and do the work that mattered to me. It wasn't an ask for money, though it was related to a job. It wasn't an ask for investment, though it was a request for someone's energy and time. It was a simple ask that redirected the trajectory of my life. It was one that I was tempted not to make because the answer could have been anything, and the answer I wanted felt like everything.

The ask was: Will you teach me?

In this chapter, I'll tell you my ask story. And while I do, I invite you to look back on your own story and notice the asks you've made, big or small, that changed something for you. But before I share about my ask that changed everything, let's hear about Linda. Maybe your ask looked a bit like hers.

> " *Notice the asks you've made, big or small, that changed something for you.* "

One sunny day, Linda the Curious was out for a walk in the neighborhood with her son. As they came around the corner, they saw a sign planted in front of a house. Not just any house—*the* house. You know, that house in the neighborhood that was built a bazillion years ago and looms large and mysterious. That house that feels like it's celebrating Halloween every day. It's not spooky, but *kinda* spooky. Nobody is sure who really lives there. Maybe ghosts? Maybe one old woman who peers out the front windows from behind the doily-ish drapes? But today, the sign planted out front of that house read "For Sale" and "Agent Tour Today. Buyer tours by appointment only."

Linda was burning with curiosity, but just stood there. Her son, however, jumped at the chance to see the inside of that beautifully creepy mansion. "Mom, let's go in," he said.

Linda brushed his suggestion away and responded, "We can't. It's an agent's tour. We're not agents."

Undeterred, her son said, "Duh. Can't we ask?"

She swallowed. Linda got that little pinch that said, *This isn't for you. Who do you think you are?* But she also got a little boost at the thought of finding out if she could satisfy her curiosity and get into that damn house, even just for five minutes.

Welcome to the ZOFO, Linda.

So Linda the Curious pushed open the gate, walked up to the looming front door, and knocked.

Her heart pounding, she waited for the listing agent to come to the door. The door swung open and the well-dressed and stern-faced agent looked down her nose at Linda and her son. "Can I help you?"

Let's get to the point. Linda asked for a walkthrough—and a walkthrough is what she got.

Linda told me this story and wrapped it up by saying, "I don't know why, but asking to get that walkthrough felt like . . . I don't know . . . like I was trespassing, but with permission. Not the tour, but the ask itself. I realize I pass on a lot of opportunities because I just assume it's not a possibility. But no! We asked and got to do something really special together. My son and I. And now I see that I can ask. I can just ask. It was ten years ago, but I was in my thirties. I don't know why this took me so long; it seems so obvious now. That experience changed everything for me. Now, I just . . . well, I just ask."

It was an ask that created an aha! moment. It was an ask that changed everything.

WILL YOU TEACH ME?

My early days were lost days. I was wandering. In college, I majored in international economics. When I graduated, it was time to get serious and go find a "real job." I'd loved my coursework, but, turns out, I hated every relevant job I interviewed for as well as, sadly, every job description related to the field. I think I just hated having a traditional "job" as my next step. I interviewed a bunch during that fall after graduation, and it was a claustrophobic experience. I distinctly remember sitting in an interview with a huge financial institution. I felt fancy in my suit and pumps (it was the late nineties/ early aughts, people, so, pumps) and sitting on the thirty-seventh floor of a big shiny building in San Francisco. But when I was sitting in the interview for an analyst position, I started to feel like I was in a pressure chamber. Walls were closing in and the room went blurry. My blouse was tightening around my throat and all I could do was wait until it was over and I'd walk (run!) out of the building while talking myself (screaming at the top of my internal lungs) off a ledge.

How in the hell am I going to do this? Have a "real job" that doesn't feel like this? I'd wonder, aghast.

Every role begged me to climb the ladder first and then get to do the thing I *really* wanted to do later on. Every job was about what you could do after that job. You'll be an analyst for a few years and then you can move into other jobs. Worse, I wasn't even sure I knew what I *really* wanted. I didn't want to believe that my only option was to hate what I'd do for a living before I could access doing what I loved.

So I decided to course correct and get super-duper clear on what I wanted, then find a path that allowed me to have just enough of what I loved inside of what was hard to motivate me to move forward. I just needed to answer two questions: (1) What do I really want to do? and (2) Where can I do it?

I embarked on a treasure hunt for the . . . loot? The booty? The trove? The pot-o-gold? The mother lode? The manna from heaven? An industry and a job I could see myself in and know, *THAT is so me! I want that.* A full body YES! The hunt went on for months. I read hundreds of job descriptions in newspapers (yes, newspapers). I went to networking events to learn about what people do. I looked at graduate programs for clues on what might be interesting to me. I booked informational interviews with salespeople and folks working in public policy. I learned about people called "ombudsmen" and about something called "fiber optics." Turns out, fiber optics were gonna be big.

Over those months I continued to teach group fitness—step aerobics, BODYPUMP, and spin classes (not quite leg warmers and G-strings, but close)—at many gyms in my county, a gig I'd held throughout college. With the instructor mic on my head, I entertained my classes by telling them about the fortunes and misfortunes on my hunt for the full body YES.

One day, Jess the Boss (she was not *my* boss; just a woman with serious boss energy), whom I'd never spoken with directly but noticed was coming regularly to my Tuesday night spin class, got off her bike at the end of class and walked toward me. She wanted to have a word. And Jess was all about business. When she talks, you listen.

She introduced herself to me and said, "I've been listening to your stories for months now. You're funny."

Thanks, Jess.

She said, "I'm an executive coach."

I'm sorry, a what? Does that have something to do with fiber optics?

". . . and my client is growing his business. He has a training company that focuses on leadership communications, and he's looking to bring in new trainers. You'd be great. I'd like to connect the two of you. I've already told him about you, so if you're open, I can make the intro this week."

Fuck. This sounds cool. Breathe, Dia, breathe.

A few weeks later, I was sitting in a restaurant in my stupid suit and pumps, starstruck by the person across from me.

Corporate training? Professional development? *WHAT THE FUCK IS THAT? I NEED TO LEARN MORE!* Executive leadership. Storytelling as a tool for business success. Helping people with public speaking? *THAT'S A THING?* It seems obvious now, but this was 1999 and I wanted to party like it. The internet was nascent and the visibility into career paths, domains, and opportunities were harder to see. This whole thing was a lucky discovery.

I sat in the conversation bright-eyed and trying to hold my shit together. There was something here. I wasn't exactly sure what it was, but I felt energized. The work sounded so fun and weirdly familiar. The way he was talking about his work was how I felt about teaching group fitness—it was about helping people step into their power.

"What's next?" I asked.

"Come to our next workshop and watch from the back of the room. After that, we can talk next steps," he said.

And so I went. The workshop was held at a training facility for a global hardware company. Like, a big, super fancy one. And the workshop itself? It. Was. Awesome.

It was a three-day workshop that brought together a bunch of finance managers who wanted to learn how to communicate better by gaining presentation skills. On day two, I got blown away. I saw people in the room, through Jedi-level facilitation, step into their power and exhibit a huge shift in how they impacted their audience and advanced their project, cause, and leadership.

I was hit with a Full. Body. YES! There have been few times in my life when I've felt so strongly that I wanted something, so singularly focused. I watched the workshop experience unfold and all I could think was, *I MUST FIND A WAY TO DO THIS WORK!*

I went home exhausted and excited, my head spinning. I'd found the loot. The booty. The pot o' gold. I'd hit the mother lode. I'd found an industry (training and development) and a job (workshop facilitator) about which

I could say, *THAT is so me. I want that!* I wanted to do what I'd seen the facilitator do in that workshop. I wanted to work for that company.

There was one problem: I was unqualified.

I had no credentials. No degree in communications, writing, or theater. No business experience, unless you count all those Saturdays of my youth when I cleaned my grandpa's insurance office in exchange for pancakes and a ten-spot. And group fitness? Not quite the same environment as the business world.

The trainers who led these workshops had years of experience. Many of them came from performance and writing backgrounds. They'd run programs for other training companies. Not me. I was green. Super green. I needed my big break.

My way in to the field was through this man's mentorship. I hoped to become an apprentice. My way in was asking him if he would teach me.

So I made the ask. And I was squarely in my Zone of Freaking Out. I pushed through the fear and made the ask anyway, willing to make a request I believed would get a no. I was prepared for full rejection, a wagging finger in my face, and a, *No, you're not ready.* But instead? He faxed (yes, faxed) me a contract and brought me on as his apprentice. A few weeks later, I was on a plane to New York and on the way to becoming the woman I am today.

As I look back, asking "Will you teach me?" is the ask that changed everything.

Like Linda the Curious, you may make a small ask that ends up showing you how asking can be a pathway to accessing opportunities you would otherwise believe are not on the menu. For me, my ask is one that materially shifted the course of my life. Thinking back on it reminds me that asking is a strategy I have in my pocket to make grand strides toward what matters to me and toward my goals.

> **Asking can be a pathway to accessing opportunities you would otherwise believe are not on the menu.**

Use the next chapters to prime yourself to think about the power of asking as a versatile, flexible, and powerful strategy for professional success. Think about the ask that gets you the visibility you need to secure that next role at your organization. Or the ask that gives you access to a network that opens doors for you. The ask that puts you more in control of your time, money, and life. The ask that can bring into balance who you are and the work you do by facilitating a career change, giving you a new skill, or helping you move into a new industry. I want you to be able to identify the asks that can make a difference in your business, career, and life. And when you go to make that ask, I hope you will ask like an auctioneer and never leave any money or opportunity on the table.

Because one ask can change everything.

IT'S JOURNAL TIME! (If you're not the journaling type, then just reflect! You can think about these questions while you're gardening, walking the dog, scrubbing the tub, or push-scootering to the corner store for an Almond Joy.)

Chances are, you've had a similar kind of aha! moment to the ones presented in this chapter—an ask that changed something in a big way. Reflecting on that moment and summoning that memory can remind you of the power you have and the impact asking can make in your life, work, business, and career. It can even work as a little pep talk when you need one.

Rest a soft gaze on your past, either recent or way back, and just scan your experiences. Use the prompts below to reflect or journal:

- What was an ask I made that changed everything?
- What did it lead to?
- What did I expect it to do for me, and what did it actually do for me?
- Looking back at it now, what can I learn from the experience?

PART II

Empower the Ask: Ideas and Strategies from the Auctioneering Stage

CHAPTER 4

Empower the Ask

Now you know how to ask like an auctioneer: ask to get a no by stepping into your ZOFO. For most of us, the ask that threatens a no inevitably lives in the ZOFO. And if what we want lives out there, how can we help ourselves wade out into that territory so we can make the asks that get us more of what we need to reach our goals? We do it by empowering our ask.

Notice I say empower *your ask*. *You* are already empowered. You're smart and capable and resourceful. I mean, just look at you right now. You're reading this book and finding the resources you need to ask for more and get it. You have all you need to nurture your asks as they grow into the hammer-wielding helpers you need them to be.

We need ideas and strategies that can encourage our internal tiny geniuses to charge, headlong, into the ZOFO to help us discover what's out there. And we'll learn these strategies together over the next several chapters.

In each of the chapters in this part, I'll be sharing an idea I took away from my experiences on the auctioneering stage paired with a strategy you can use to implement that idea in a way that moves you enthusiastically, or at least solidly, into your ZOFO. You may not use all of them, but be on the lookout for that one of the nine that strikes you right and works as a zinger of an idea you can use as a strategy to ask for more. The point of each of these ideas is to arm your asks with what they need so they become the most powerful version possible. With your help, your asks will be more ready for action themselves, armed with a plan and the clarity they need to storm the castle. And they won't feel alone.

Throughout the part ahead, I'll share stories from my own life and from other women I've met who've used these ideas and strategies to ask for more and get it. While I've anonymized each of the stories, they are stories of real women in real situations who challenged what they thought they could get, asked like an auctioneer, and, by doing so, changed everything.

One nuance to call out here: Not all asks you'll make are ZOFO asks. You won't ask like an auctioneer *every* time you ask for something. Many asks you'll make will be "please pass the salt" asks. But when you're making an ask that is materially important to moving you into your next phase? That's when I hope you'll ask like an auctioneer and use one or more of the ideas in this book to help you do it. I want you to use the ideas and strategies in this section for

> " *Arm your asks with what they need so they become the most powerful version possible.* "

those pivotal and strategic moments along the path to your goal, such as that critical year when it's time to raise your rates in your service-based business, that job change that will level up your salary or benefits or title or visibility, that pitch you can make to get on a bigger stage or gain access to a better network.

The ideas in these chapters are simple and even work secondhand, so if a strategy strikes you as particularly helpful or applicable, tell a friend about it. And when you do, you'll be having an impact aligned with the purpose of this book. The email below is from a woman I met just once at a fundraising gala but who has learned about the ideas I'm about to share through a shared connection. She got the ideas secondhand, but she has used them to make first-rate asks that have had a big impact.

She is a red-hot lawyer who was looking to level up her career as in-house counsel to a badass company. I'd heard some tidbits from our community of mutual friends that she'd been using Ask Like an Auctioneer strategies, and had successfully moved into her own place for the first time in her life (Yay! No more housemates!). She'd gotten a foothold financially as a result of asking for more over time. So when I got this email, I knew exactly who it was, and I couldn't have felt more grateful for the experience of auctioneering, which allowed me to learn these lessons and pass them along to her and to you.

—

Hi Dia -- I'm Mickel's friend, Arden! We met a few years ago, and you taught me a lot in that short time about asking for more.

Since then, I've negotiated two different job offers and leveled up in both. I just accepted a job offer this afternoon where I negotiated a $10K signing bonus directly from my ZOFO.

As a result, I would like to use a portion of that bonus to make a donation in your name to a charity of your choice. I would not have access to this abundance if not for you, and I cannot wait to spread the wealth. Please let me know where to send the check. xoxoxoxo*

—

What a beautiful example of the kind of impact I want this book to have on you and for you. Arden put more money and decision-making power in her own hands, and boom! She's thrilled to share her success.

Learn these ideas once, and use them forever. They're designed to be simple, fun, and accessible. You may make use of one of them, all of them, or a combo of a few. Maybe you'll adapt one to make it your own and to make it work best for you—great!

---

* Email has been edited for clarity and anonymity.

With a strong bias toward action, and with my heart in my hand, my hope is that these ideas help get *you* into action in ways that stretch you but are aligned with who you are. You are smart about your situation, wise about who you are, bold in your ambitions, and courageous just by picking up this book.

In my leadership communications coaching practice, I often tell my clients that while we are going to have a lot of fun in our work together, I take very seriously what we're working on. I do not take lightly that a founder I'm working with is deep in the thrill and fear of taking a $120 million investment and fulfilling the promises that come with that. Or that a newly minted CEO is putting herself on the line as she leads an organization into its next phase. Or for you to be making an ask that can materially change the status of your goal-getting, no matter how big or small it might seem. I know it's big to you.

Let's empower that ask, together.

CHAPTER 5

People Are Irrational

Idea: People are irrational, or *their* rationale is not *your* rationale.

Strategy: Don't decide for your audience what they'll say "yes" and "no" to. Let them decide.

In every auction I've done, things don't go as planned. When I was just getting started auctioneering, I was really concerned about what an item *should* go for. We love to speculate, and we love to have a rationale for what we think an item—in auctioneering we call it a "lot"—will sell for. That estimating makes us feel a little bit in control, like we get to decide what happens because we've already gamed it out, predicted the outcome, and built a rationale for what someone should pay and why they should pay it.

Over time, I've let go of that inclination to predict. I've just been surprised too many times. Once in the midst of the auction, all that storytelling we've done about this lot or that lot and who should bid and how much it'll go for just disappears—there's just the ask, and the response. That's it.

I remember encountering one particularly intimidating lot in an auction I did in the first year of auctioneering.

> **"There's just the ask, and the response. That's it."**

The executive director told me, "Ten thousand dollars. That's what it's worth," in our preparations for the fundraiser. It was a piece of art—a daguerreotype, which is a sort of photograph produced via a special process using "iodine-sensitized silver plate and mercury vapor," whatever the hell that is. This artist was well established in his craft and had a reputation. Just looking at it, although it was small, I could feel the energy and expectation around this piece. It almost vibrated as it hung there waiting to be sold in the auction, staring at me with furrowed brows and piercing eyes that said, *I WILL SELL FOR $10,000.* I tried to avoid looking at it directly all night.

When it was time to take it off the wall and sell it at the live auction, I took a breath and opened the bid at an easy $1,800. Knowing the gallery owners were there and the staff was full of anticipation at what the item would sell for (*TEN THOUSAND DOLLARS!!!*), I quickly and methodically moved through the opening bid and up in increments to see who would stay in and who would fall off the bidding. Within seventy-nine seconds, the bidding slowed. I fought to keep the energy high in my performance while the concentration of raised bidding paddles in the room thinned out. It was clear that we were down to two bidders more quickly than we had anticipated. I could feel myself squarely in my ZOFO as I made the final asks to see where the ceiling was and boom, in less than two minutes we'd gone from opening bid to winning bid. The item sold for an underwhelming $6,200. We had a rationale about what the item would go for; the people in the room did not share the same rationale.

IT CAN GO THE OTHER WAY

At another auction, I stood on the stage in an outdoor tent where the clanking of banquet utensils and the high hum of dinner party chatter and laughter swelled to fill the area. A large community of a few hundred people committed to land stewardship and the preservation of open space had come together to fundraise for one of the most important park conservancies on the West Coast. It was time to begin the auction, and I couldn't let the chaos and fun of the activity in the tent hold the fundraising we were about to do hostage.

In our preparations for the event, we analyzed each lot, telling stories and building rationales about what would sell at what price and what we could and might expect from the crowd. We played it out in our minds and locked in our predictions just enough to have a set of assumptions we thought were solid. We'd kinda decided what was gonna happen.

Then came lot five. I opened the bid, not expecting to go much over twice the opening bid, which was a cool $5,000. As the increments went up, I approached the number we thought it would max out at and in the same breath blew right past it. In under two minutes, I sold a one-night glamping trip (fancy camping) for $55,000 . . . twice. One party bought it at that number, and another party said, "Us too!" and boom, we'd sold it twice, and each time for more than double what we thought it would sell for.

On the outside, it all looked so irrational. And, often, people seemingly make decisions in ways that are unpredictable and "irrational." Over and over again, I *cannot* predict or decide what someone else is going to pay for any item I auction. I've tried! But I've given up. I have *zero* idea what their response will be to my requests for a bid. My job can't be to decide for them what they'll pay; my job is to ask and find out.

Often when I talk about this out in the world, some folks balk, saying, "People are not irrational!" and "We make data-driven decisions." Bullshit. Even if that's sometimes true, whether at a business-strategy level or in our personal decisions tied to relationships, values, and goals, we very often go with our guts. We find alternatives to the "data-driven decisions" because we like something or someone or the conditions are just right enough to break the rules. It's not useful to push aside the fact that our guts are loud, or even for me to try to know what my audience's guts are saying to them! Instead, my only job is to ask and find out.

If you really can't accept the whole emotions-drive-decision-making thing, try this: *Their* rationale is not *your* rationale. Their rationale for what someone may say yes or no to is not, or may not be, your rationale. So stop deciding for people what their response will be. Be smart about asking, but let go of deciding for them.

If every time I opened a bid I decided ahead of time what someone should pay for something, I'd leave bazillions of dollars on the table. I truly thought the glamping trip would go for, say, $25,000. That seemed like enough. But if I'd shouted "SOLD!" when I hit that number? I would have left a shit ton of value just sitting on the table, winking at me.

The no is the destination you're striving toward, not the yes you think they'll go for. Because your rationale is not their rationale. Butt out, and ask and find out what you can get instead of guessing, because you'll very likely be wrong. Use irrationality and unpredictability to your advantage by expecting the unexpected.

This idea is super useful as you start to plan your ask. You'll begin to notice you're telling yourself all kinds of stories about how they'll respond and pretty soon, your ask is limited by all those machinations. You've already decided how it's gonna go, and yet you can't really be sure. Instead, if you lean on this notion—that people are irrational and it's none of your business to decide for them—you free yourself to ask and see how it goes.

I mean, just look at all those irrational decisions hanging in your closet. And by the way, I know about that irrational decision to buy that cocktail dress you'll never wear. And I know you don't have any regrets about it. You love that thing and it was so fun to buy! It may have been irrational but you sure-as-shit had and have a rationale for why you bought it. We love to justify our decisions even if it's with "I wanted it, OK?!" and we will defend our decisions to the death of our bank accounts, business strategies, and bunkhouses full of crap we don't need.

> **Use irrationality and unpredictability to your advantage by expecting the unexpected.**

APPLYING THIS IDEA AND STRATEGY

Use this idea to help you step into your ZOFO and ask for more than you think you can get, even if it's just a little more. If you can use this idea of "people are irrational or their rationale is not your rationale" to take the pressure off of feeling like you need to know before you know, you'll be better able to ask without being attached to the outcome. You may find that you can make the asks that let you be surprised.

Amber had had enough. Living with housemates, this grown ass lawyer was ready to have a grown ass apartment all to herself, but she needed to be able to afford it. She dreamt of waking up in a quiet apartment and making coffee in a kitchen in which everything was just as she left it the night before. Amber was smart, didn't live outside her means, and knew that this year, her job search would be for the one that allowed her to move out of roommate life and into a life that reflected her priorities.

After a long few months of job seeking, she'd made it through a series of interviews with an organization that was the right fit for her, and she was now in salary negotiation.

Squarely in her ZOFO, Amber drew on the idea that "their rationale is not my rationale" and instead of making a salary ask she thought *they* would find "reasonable," she decided to ask for more and find out from them what their limits were.

She asked big. Big enough to make her skin feel hot. Big enough to make her feel alive. Big enough for her to know she was challenging her own assumptions.

(A quick note on *big*: your big is not my big. Amber's big is not your big. Big is relative. Big is personal. Big, in this book, is not absolute—it's subjective and contextual. For my daughter, big is asking for a private desk in her classroom during reading time so she can reduce distractions. For you, big might be a 5 percent raise. So when I describe big asks in this book, just imagine it's big for whoever the story is about. And stand up for your big, because your big is yours. Your ZOFO is yours. There is no right or wrong; there's only bigger than you're used to, and a ZOFO only you can feel.)

Amber submitted her salary request and after confirmation of receipt, her prospective new employer went . . . dark. Lights out. For days.

Amber was *sure* she was being laughed out of the building. But no. A few days later, the lights came on, and Amber got what she asked for.

Did she get a no? Nope. Did she get more than she thought she would? Yep. Why? Because she aimed for a no by recognizing that her rationale and their rationale were not the same, which gave her the courage to step into her ZOFO and make the ask to find out what *they'd* say yes to.

CHAPTER 6

Know Your Reserve

Idea: Know your reserve.

Strategy: Always identify the minimum you'll accept so *you* know exactly what *you'll* say "yes" and "no" to.

L ife jackets are great.

If you belly flop or get the wind knocked out of you when you jump, you'll float. You can trust them. When I was little, every summer my grandparents took me and my cousin up to Lake Shasta in Northern California to spend a few days on a houseboat. A houseboat is like a motor home (or caravan, depending on where you're from), but on the water. Lake Shasta is a huge, cold lake at the foot of Mount Shasta, which stands 3,500 feet tall and is capped with a big white glacier peering down at its namesake body of water. Lake Shasta is where I learned to jump off the side of a boat into open water. Intimidating and thrilling, tossing myself overboard was a big sign I was growing up. And I could do it because I wore a life jacket. My life jacket fit right, was the perfect shape, and gave me the confidence to jump. I knew that no matter what happened, I'd float. And then, I could decide what to do next. Swim out a bit? Yell for my cousin to jump in after me? Swim around to the back of the boat and crawl up the ladder all by myself?

That life jacket meant that I could work up from a pencil dive holding my nose all the way to a full flailing 720° spin from the railing, screaming from the top of my lungs, arms held out to my sides, and eyes closed until I was under the surface of that icy green water. That lifejacket let me say yes to seeing what was possible and then put me in control of my next step.

Reserves are kinda like that.

YOUR RESERVE PUTS YOU IN CONTROL

Your reserve is the absolute minimum you'll accept in any negotiation. In auctioneering, a reserve is the minimum bid I'd accept for a particular lot. Sometimes, our reserve is zero dollars, other times it's any number above that. The reserve amount you set is your choice. For example, you might ask for $5,000 for that junker car you're selling, but you'd take less—but no less than $3,800. That $3,800 is your reserve.

> **"**
> *Your reserve is the absolute minimum you'll accept in any negotiation.*
> **"**

In auctioneering, we identify a reserve for everything we sell. I'll ask my client: What is the minimum price you'll take at auction for this lot, or that one? And we decide together. If we are selling something on consignment, we need the reserve to be some acceptable amount above what the nonprofit needs to carve out for the seller. But if we're selling a donated lot and the donor doesn't have a stake in what it fetches at auction, we'll have a reserve of zero even if we start the bidding at one dollar.

Either way, *before* I step into a live auction, we've decided on the reserve for each lot we'll sell. When we know that, we know we'll get at least what we need and nothing less.

Having reserves is a wildly powerful tool for me when I'm on stage taking bids, as I don't have to make any decisions, right there in the heat of the moment, about whether to sell an item or not. I'm protected against being manipulated in the moment or situation, because we've already decided what we'll accept.

Because I'm safe, I can go into the bidding with curiosity and delight around what is about to happen, letting go of an attachment to a certain outcome because I know that people are irrational. I won't know what they'll say yes or no to, but I know where *my* boundary is.

So what do I do if none of the bids meet my reserve? Great question!

In an auctioneering context, if we've opened the bidding on a particular item below the reserve (which we do to get bidding going) and no bids come in to meet or exceed the reserve, I have a couple of choices. I can just say "pass" and move on to the next lot. The item didn't sell, so I take a pass, and the show continues. Or, we can be a little more elegant about it, and when the bidding audience doesn't meet the reserve, a "house" bid goes up and we "sell" it back to the house for what looks like a price but is really just a bid that we declare as the winner in order to take the item off the table. This lets the lot go back to the organization in a graceful way that doesn't break the rhythm of the exchange I'm having with the audience and lets everyone save face. Either way, none of that is accidental and we've planned for the scenario and have already decided what we'll do if we don't meet our reserve.

Already decided.

YOU HAVE CHOICES

But you're not in a live auction. You're in your life and career and business.

Here are the great questions I get all the time: "But what if *I* get a NO? What should I do?" My answer? I don't know! What *are* you gonna do? I can't wait to hear!

There's nothing you're *supposed* to do when your reserve isn't met. Only what you *want* to do. And you get to decide.

> **There's nothing you're supposed *to do when your reserve isn't met. Only what you* want *to do. And you get to decide.*

You get to decide.

So, what *are* you going to do? If you have a plan, then you won't be held hostage by the response you receive.

If they say no, you get to decide what you do next. Here's a little list of examples, but make up your own that work for you:

- Quit.
- Engage them in a conversation about what else you could do together.
- Ask for a referral.
- Take yourself off the market.
- Walk away.
- Say thank you.
- Say no, thank you.
- Say fuck you.
- Change the scope of the project.
- Do a little dance.
- Take yourself out for brunch.
- Give them feedback.
- Give them no feedback.
- Ask someone else for what you need.
- Go back to school.
- Take a painting class.
- Inquire about what has them saying no even to your reserve.
- Gather feedback via a survey.
- Call your best friend and cry.
- Move on.

You get to decide.

But the power comes with already deciding your reserve and already deciding what you'll do if you don't get it.

Knowing your reserve will help you feel and be powerful, and step into that almighty ZOFO with confidence.

APPLYING THIS IDEA AND STRATEGY

Chelsea the Move-Maker was ready to make a move—up, or out. But she didn't realize it until she got real with herself.

She was heads down working on her Ask Plan (see chapter eighteen for guidance on building yours) in a workshop and raised her hand when it was time to share.

"OK, my goal is to be a people manager in the next twelve months. I've been promised this is my future here for quarter after quarter and it's just not happened yet. So this time, I'm gonna really ask. Like, really, really."

But that ask plan wasn't clear enough. We needed to know some specifics because there was a chance she could continue to get breadcrumbed (led on for too long) on this. So we asked her:

"How many people do you want to manage? Like, what counts? Do you need a big team? A few folks? Get specific."

"I would like two to start. With a budget and plan to grow the team to five in the first twelve months."

Now we're on to something. "Great. But when? When would you like this?"

"Soon," she said.

"What is soon?"

"By the end of the next quarter," she said. All sure and whatnot.

So we had to ask. "Based on the pattern of behavior so far,

there's a chance they'll keep breadcrumbing you. What's the absolute latest deadline you'll accept this change materializing for you? What's your reserve?"

Chelsea the Move-Maker gulped.

"One quarter after that. That's it," she replied, her eyes wide. She was actually saying it. Drawing a line. That was her reserve. I wanted to find out just how reserve-ish it was.

"What if you don't get it by that drop-dead date? Then what?" I asked quietly.

She took a breath. "I'll leave. It'll be time for me to leave." She looked sad but relieved. Just knowing where she stood was a revelation for her. But in that moment, Chelsea the Move-Maker had decided what mattered to her, taken a stand, and defined a boundary so that the situation couldn't hold her back from her dreams with false promises and aspirations the organization just couldn't make good on in the timeline that matched up with the plan Chelsea had for herself.

There is so much power in that clarity. She chose her reserve then, and knowing what her next move would be if her reserve wasn't met gave her the confidence and clarity to ask for the management position she knew was the next step for her career.

CHAPTER 7

Increments Matter

Idea: Increments matter.

Strategy: Don't just split the difference on the dollars. Plan your increments, and know what increments you have to plan.

I opened the bid at $1,200.

People in the audience raised their paddles at that price (a raised paddle means whoever is holding that paddle is willing to pay that price). There were so many paddles in the air that I asked for the next bid of $1,400. With many paddles still in the air, I quickly continued to raise the price in $400 increments. Soon we were at $3,400 and the paddles were reduced to only a few.

I kept going. A man at the front had raised his paddle at $3,800. I extended my hand to indicate he was the top bidder and kept going.

"I've got $3,800 looking for $4,200. Who's in at $4,200?" One woman raised her paddle at $4,200. She was in at $4,200. So I kept going.

"I've got $4,200 looking for $4,600," I looked at the man near the front.

"She's got it at forty-two, I'm looking for forty-six," I repeated. With his paddle in his lap, he stared at me. I repeated: "She's got it at forty-two," with my hand stretched toward her. "I'm looking for forty-six," extending my other hand at him. Nothing.

I'd been working in $400 increments. It was time to experiment. So I backed down by one hundred to see if he'd be in there.

"Forty-five sir. Are you in at forty-five?" His paddle went up.

"He's in at forty-five. I'm looking for forty-six." The woman raised her paddle at forty-six.

Great. Hundreds it is.

Working in one hundred dollar increments I moved forward.

"Forty-six. Looking for forty-seven." He raised his paddle.

"He's got it at forty-seven. Forty-eight?" She was in.

"Forty-nine, are you in at forty-nine, sir?" Yes. He was.

"Five?" She was in.

"Fifty-one. Are you in at fifty-one, sir?" He stared back at me. Paddle down. He was out.

I asked one more time.

"Fifty-one. She's got it at $5,000. I'm looking for a $5,100 bid. Are you in or are you out, sir?" The room watched. He shook his head subtly. He was out. I got a no. I knew where the ceiling was and quickly turned to the winning bidder and said, "Sold. Sold for $5,000 to paddle number 103."

I've learned from auctioneering that increments matter. In this case, the man bidding was in at $3,800, out at $4,600 (when I was using $400 increments), back in at $4,500 when he heard I was moving to $100 increments, and then he stayed in until $4,900. He blew past the original number he'd said no to because things had changed—we were taking an approach using smaller increments. Do I know why that mattered to him? Nope. Do I care? Nope. I just know that increments matter.

When I move through an auction and choose my increments, I'm responding to what's going on in the room and negotiating with the audience to see where we can go together. Sometimes, I make a jump that's too big, say, $500, and sometimes I'll back down by $300, and then bidding picks up, and I blow right past the number I was at when I was using $500 increments. Sometimes we can bundle. Bundling can sound something like, "If you take this *and* that, and pick both up by Friday, you'll get this price."

Everyone can play in increments as they define what they're willing to negotiate and what they're not. And sometimes you may add value (increments) that wasn't even on the table when you started. Great!

KNOW WHAT TO INCREMENT

Money is easy. It's dollars and cents. Or, euros. Or if you're in Ghana, it's cedi. But there are other increments you can play with, even in the asks that are not directly money related. You can incrementally negotiate for things that will help you reach your goals, things you can ask for more or less of or different combinations of. If you're gonna give me less time on stage, I want to sit next to Barbara Streisand or Venus Williams at the awards dinner. I'll take sharing a byline if we do a video interview where I talk about the portion of the story I worked on. No? How about I'm the voice-over for the promotion of the project and I'm happy to be the third name in the byline order. Things like that—create new things you can ask for in increments.

Other things you can increment can include:

- Time—add or subtract time
- Participation—increase or decrease your level of participation
- Creating something—determine what you will make or not make
- Flexibility—iron out how much flexibility you have in the terms of your agreement
- Components of a process—decide what you'll do and what they'll do
- Credit (the "finance" kind)—name how much or little of it you want or need
- Credit (the "who-gets-it" kind) request how much visibility or credit you get
- Shares/Restricted Stock Units (RSU)—request more shares or fewer

- Title change—choose your preferred title (Manager, Sr. Manager, Head of . . ., Lead . . ., etc.)
- Audience/stage size—seek a small, medium, or large; virtual or live
- Responsibilities—take ownership of something or nothing
- Availability—determine how available (or not) you are
- Role—delineate what role you play on a team or project despite your job title
- Where you are seated at an important event (protocol stuff; trust me, it's a thing)—leverage this to increase social status and networking
- Time on the mic—choose how much spotlight you get

The list goes on and on, and may include things that aren't so obvious. Things that aren't on the menu and things you invent that are important to you.

Even in my own work, I've added items and increments into the mix that mattered to me, that helped me say yes to less of something (while still above my reserve) because I also got something else that was valuable to me. These increments can work together.

Often, when I make an ask and the conversation goes into increments, I'll introduce new items and new increments that feel ZOFO-ish to me and that feel like a positive surprise to the other party. More than once I've heard, "Wow! I hadn't thought of that. That's important to you?"

And I get more of what matters to me and can play in increments that aren't so limited to all or nothing. When multiple amounts of different things are at play, you have more room to negotiate your ask incrementally. Know the things you can increment. And then increment them.

APPLYING THIS IDEA AND STRATEGY

Plan your increments and know what increments are available to plan for. After a few auctions, I started to notice where the increments are in every negotiation. As you look at the asks you'll make, take some time to inventory all the components of what you're asking for, how they relate to one another, and what kind of increments you want to operate with.

There is no guaranteed "right" increment, but taking time to consider which ones make sense for you and which

> " *Know the things you can increment. And then increment them.* "

ones you'll work with will help put you in control and prevent jumping directly to your reserve if you get a "no" to your ZOFO number.

If you have multiple components to an ask, sketch out your different scenarios that let you know what combinations of each component could be possible and what you consider your reserve for each combination.

For example, you could combine salary, benefits, time off, flex work time, and bonus all as a combination of things to increment. If I get more flex time, I'd be OK with less time off, or I'd take a lower salary for a bigger benefits package, and so on.

Freelancer? Maybe your increments are around scope of project, rate, the ability to profile your client in a case study or white paper or similar content, introductions or membership to a client network, co-publishing an article to elevate the visibility of your work, and a bonus for coming in early and on budget. Increment up and down using all you have. How do you increment a white paper? Maybe at the first ask it's an in-depth booklet with video interviews of users and you can increment it down to a one-pager. Between those two extremes there are all kinds of possibilities.

Who knows! You get to make up what you want to put on the table to increment.

To demonstrate this idea in action, let's take the story of Micha the Star, a woman who almost gave away the farm, but who didn't—thanks to incrementing.

Micha the Star was in the audience for one of my keynotes. She reached out to me later and wanted some help. She was a rising star in the advertising world, moving from her current agency to a new one, and struggling to put together her salary and total compensation ask. She didn't want to lowball herself. She wanted to ask like an auctioneer. When we first spoke, I asked her what she wanted, and she shared her salary ask: $72,000 a year. But she didn't stop there. She added that she wanted flex time, three weeks off per year, and other perks. Great! Go, Micha!

When I asked her salary reserve, she said $64,000. Then I asked her what her ZOFO number was for her salary. You know, the one she *thinks* might get her a no. She said she thought it'd be $86,000. Just saying that out loud made her realize she wanted to ask for $86,000, just to see if that was the ceiling. Now for the kicker: I asked her what she'd do if she got a "no." She said, "Well, I'd counteroffer $72,000."

But what about all the increments between $86,000 and $72,000? What about the combinations? Would Micha the Star take $82,000 if she gave up a week of vacation or moved her ask from two flex days per week to one? Could she increment with $78,000 if she got a little more in her health savings account contribution? Or a professional development budget? There are lots of increments to consider and combinations of those increments. Recognize those, and do some planning in advance. It will prevent you from giving away the farm at the first sign of resistance to your ask.

And Micha the Star? She got a "no" at $86,000, but landed on a number that was above her money reserve *and* included all the right combinations of her other items in her bundle. She's now got a title of copywriter, no longer "junior copywriter," and got more because she recognized all the increments and their combinations that mattered.

CHAPTER 8

Are You In, or Are You Out?

Idea: Are you in, or are you out?

Strategy: Make people decide so you know where you stand and can move on.

S ometimes, you gotta know when to move on.

How? Find out if they're in or if they're out. When your ask has been on the table for a while—maybe for too long—you've got to be willing to apply a little pressure to get the ask unblocked or to unblock yourself.

I promised you that this book would be about ways you can ask for more and get it using what I've learned from my impact hobby of auctioneering. This chapter's strategy isn't so much about making the ask as it is about getting an ask unstuck.

> **Be willing to apply a little pressure to get the ask unblocked or to unblock yourself.**

You've got plans. You've got goals. You've got deadlines, and you've got dreams. In this chapter, I'll share a little idea I learned and have used on stage. I now use it in my own negotiations to know where I stand in order to get things unstuck so I can get on with it.

In chapter seven, when we talked about how increments matter, I told the story of an auction where we danced around at an ask of $5,100. I asked it a few times and eventually, looking at an indecisive bidder who had been with us from $3,800, but who was now hesitant and giving me a little side-eye, signaling hesitancy, I cleared it right up with a simple request for information: "I'm looking for a $5,100 bid. Are you in or are you out, sir?"

I needed to know where we stood. I've got things to do, shit to take care of, I have four more lots to sell, and I can't wait around all day for your ass. Kindly.

"Are you in? Or are you out, sir?"

I could see him feel the pressure to decide, and he did—with a little smile, he pressed his lips together and shook his head in a way that said, *I'm out.*

Oh, thank goddess. Thanks for letting me know.

"Sold. Sold for $5,000 to paddle number 103." Done.

You will get stuck too. Maybe because that boss who's promised you that bonus can't seem to tell you if it's actually coming, so you stall that deposit on your first apartment where that second bedroom will turn into your studio from which you'll be launching your new podcast tied to your dream to build a community around women and adventure travel, which will lead to launching your travel company once you've got an audience who are so fucking committed to you and your idea that they'll be your inaugural cohort for your very first trip, who will then become brand ambassadors in building a global adventure travel company introducing millions of women to the life-changing experience of backcountry wilderness, kayaking uncharted waters, and spearfishing, all while making a pile of cash doing what you love.

Bruh, you're holding me hostage with this bonus thing.

Think of the countless moments when YOU JUST NEED TO KNOW ALREADY, GODDAMNIT!

And I *know* that most of the time—or a lot of the time, or, fine, maybe only once, but it was super-duper important at that time—you really want to find out how to get them to say yes after a long stretch of silence or stalling. So you say nothing at all, and wait.

And the clock ticks.

What if it's a no when you ask them if they're in or out? Great! Now you know where you stand and you can make a plan and get into action again. You can say to yourself, *The bonus was a no. So, I'm going to negotiate with the landlord to see if I can pay the deposit over three months*, so that you can continue working toward your goals. (That shit happens. I should know; I did it for my tenants for a rental home we had a decade ago. Why? Cuz I loved them and I saw their situation and the housing market was crazy and, IDK, I'm irrational. You might not have done that, but my rationale is not your rationale. See what I did there?)

I want you to take back control, and you do that by knowing where you stand and getting back into action, on your terms.

So, "Are you in? Or are you out, sir?"

Over and over in auctioneering, I see this question unstick a stuck bid. And since I began sharing this idea, I've heard women use it to get unstuck with their boss, their team, or a new client. You can too.

So next time you're stuck, put it out there: "Are you in? Or are you out?"

SILENCE IS GOLDEN

Perhaps you're thinking, *But I've asked where it stands, Dia! And I get met with silence!*

Take silence as a no. You ain't got time.

In an auction, I get to decide. I'm the boss of the thing. And you're the boss of your path to your goals. Yes, I know you're not working in some isolated context where you have personal control over every fucking thing—there are

> **Take silence as a no. You ain't got time.**

interdependencies. We navigate life in relationship with and to others. But you get to decide what you do with the reactions, or lack of reaction, you get to your asks. You get to respond using your own response rules.

When I auctioneer, I get to decide to take silence as a no. I get to decide whether I let people know how I'm reading their silence. I get to decide how long I'll wait with the silence before I just sell it to someone else. I get to decide.

You can too.

One woman in a workshop raised her hand. She said she needed her "boss to get off the fence" on an issue around her career path. She was clearly frustrated and demoralized, and while she wasn't on the verge of tears, I could hear the tearful anger way back at the rear of her super smart, technically excellent, data-focused, leader-ly throat. It had been going on for too long. The silence. The stalling. What felt to her like disrespect.

I asked her, "What happens if you take that silence, that stalling, as a no?"

Immediately, her energy lifted, and she had ideas.

"Well, I'd . . ." and she listed a slew of next moves she could make. She could get back into action.

When I asked her what it was like for her to take silence as a no, she replied, "A relief."

Cuz she ain't got time.

The question, then, is how much silence equals a no? Two days' worth? Five weeks? An hour? It's up to you. In my case in a fundraising auction, I'll ask a bidder three times if they'd like to bid at a certain number, and if there's silence, I'll sell it to the other bidder. If they look like they're thinking about it, I'll ask "Are you in, or are you out?" and if I'm met with silence then? I'll just say, "I'll take that as a no, thank you," and move on to the winning bidder.

BREADCRUMBING IS THE SIGN

You get to decide when to move on.

You get to decide when you ask if they're in or if they're out. You get to decide.

Breadcrumbing is one way you can recognize if it's time to ask "In or out?" or if it's time to take their silence and stalling as a no.

Remember from chapter six that "breadcrumbing" is when someone is stringing you along for too long, but giving you just enough of a little morsel of hope that you keep waiting. There's a difference between the type of waiting that comes from having a few exchanges that push a decision or answer out and the type that comes from full-on breadcrumbing. The difference is that breadcrumbing keeps you on the hook without the payoff.

And you don't have time for that.

So if you notice you're getting breadcrumbed, it might be time to take back control and get the clarity you need.

It's the tension *before* the clarity that's torture. And the thing that slows it all the fuck down.

So break that suspense for yourself. Get unstuck. And pop the question: "Are you in? Or are you out?"

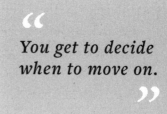

" You get to decide when to move on. "

APPLYING THIS IDEA AND STRATEGY

This seems redundant, but for the sake of clarity, I'm gonna line it out one more time: Next time you've made a big ask, and you're breadcrumbed for just too long, drop that "Are you in, or are you out?" question. And if you're met with silence? Take it as an "I'm out," and move the fuck on. Get back into action in a way that puts you in control of what's next.

Svetlana the Starter marched right up to me after a keynote I gave at a conference like we were old friends (or like I was in trouble) and stuck her hand out for a shake. Turns out, she'd been in one of my virtual keynote audiences the year before and was a fan of everything Ask Like an Auctioneer.

She didn't come to ask me a question. She came to tell me a story in her beautiful Eastern European accent, with an aliveness I couldn't ignore.

"You know that thing you talk about? In or out?"

"Yes!" I said, waiting for her to tell me it was bullshit. Because you know, haters.

"Ohmygod, Dia. Last year I had this client, right? And I had made an offer on this house for him, I'm his agent, and so, well, we got a counteroffer. And the clock was ticking. But he just kinda ghosted me for a bit, then couldn't make a decision, and I was, like, totally freaking out because it was the perfect place for him, and the price was right, and I'm a new agent, and the commission was going to be so important to me, and I was just, you know, really wanting to get unstuck with him and so excited and at the same time really worried."

"Yeeees...go on..." I prompted with that deep, dastardly voice that says, *I'm interested*.

"Anyway, I didn't know what to do. The deal felt like it was just sitting there. And he wouldn't call me back."

"Hmmmmhmmmmm?" More *tell me more* tone.

"But then I remembered the whole 'Are you in? Or are you out?' thing, and, well, I called him and asked him that very question and put a timeline on it. And guess what?"

I was totally guessing.

"He called me back and just said, 'I'm in.'"

"Yay!" I said, like we're twelve. "Did the deal close?"

"It did!" She said. "But that's not the part I wanted to tell you about. I just, well, in that moment I just found that I could take control. It was like I just found my voice in my brand-new business.

I was totally in my ZOFO, and it was great. I had the power to get it unstuck and handle any answer I got. I have the confidence now to move things forward. And this time, the deal closed, next time, maybe not, but I just don't feel like I'm at the mercy of the client anymore. I can just make a move."

And *that* is what I'm talking about.

Macie the Engineer can't take it anymore. She's is a well-respected, influential, and friendly engineering leader at an entertainment technology company many of you know and use. She was leading a big project at the company with a cross-functional team of folks who'd opted into the project. She'd recruited members from a wide set of talent from various engineering functions, and the project had kicked off weeks before.

But it was stuck in first gear. Macie was frustrated and was getting breadcrumbed by the team. There was stalling and a lot of *I'll get to it soon* energy, so Macie gathered the team in a large conference room.

She popped—or rather, dropped—the question, right in the middle of the table.

"Either you're in, or you're out. Tell me now."

She found out who was in, and who was out, and whoever didn't give a clear answer, she took as being out.

She created clarity and reshuffled the team and its priorities, added resources where the project needed it, and those who remained were off to the races.

Good job, Macie.

CHAPTER 9

Price Is a Measure
of Value, Not Worth

Idea: Price is a measure of value, not of absolute worth.

Strategy: Read the response you get to an ask as a measure of how the person you are asking values something, not as a measure of its absolute worth. Do this as a way to gain some distance and perspective on the asks you make and the noes you get so they can be and feel less personal.

I f you're a living, breathing human who participates in modern society, you've undoubtedly heard the phrases "Get paid what you're worth!" and "Know your worth!" Someone may have shouted them at you, or you may have shouted them at yourself. And yes, I want you to do both of those things! I want you to get the amount of money or recognition or power you need to reach your goals in a way that is aligned to your worth and your worthiness. I want you to ask for more and get it. I want you to be honest about exactly what you want and never settle for less. I want you to be able to ask for more every time you ask for anything at all.

Unfortunately, those worth-related catchphrases might not help you do any of these things. In fact, they often have the opposite effect of their well-meaning intent. Instead of empowering you to ask boldly, they may cause you to shift focus to obsessively evaluating your "worth." Instead of giving you confidence and clarity, they may create self-doubt. It's a nasty little mental rabbit hole that I've seen many smart women tumble down, and this chapter is my way of protecting you from taking that dark and counter-productive trip yourself.

If you've already taken that tumble, however, know that you're not alone. Far from it.

I've talked to hundreds of women about the phrase "get what you're worth," and they've been brutally honest about how it has affected them. Many pointed out that when we ask for what we believe we're worth and get a concrete reply from someone else, we think their reply is an accurate definition of our worth ("If I ask for X, and I don't get it, I must not be worth X"). We inadvertently load up the ask or negotiation with deep, personal meaning. After we've done that a few times and ground down our confidence to a tiny nub, we recalibrate our asks so there's less risk of getting a "no" (or some other answer that diminishes our self-worth). Working from a place of fear and doubt, we craft asks that leave money and opportunity on the table. We step out of our ZOFO and carve down our asks to yield guaranteed yeses.

And that's not all that's wrong with the idea of "getting what you're worth"! When we only ask for what we believe we're worth, we never stretch far enough to see what's actually possible. Women have been socially con-ditioned to believe that we shouldn't take up so much space or brag or be proud and loud about our accomplishments. This means that far too many of us have deeply skewed ideas of what we're truly worth. The asks we make fall short of getting what we need and deserve because we have no real idea of how talented, valuable, and visionary we are. We don't allow ourselves to see those dazzling versions of ourselves, and our shortsightedness hinders our ability to ask for more.

It's shitty that these simple catchphrases—designed to help us step up and play bigger—leave us hamstrung and underpowered, right? Luckily, there's an alternative, and I'm here to tell you what it is. Once I really, truly understood how negotiations play out on the auctioneering stage—where, in real and rapid time, I witnessed the gap between how I might value something and how buyers in the room valued it—I saw a way to reframe what something is "worth." I saw an opportunity to recast "worth" in a way that lowers the stakes enough to raise them. I saw a way to help women take it all less personally so we could feel more freedom and confidence around every ask we make. Let me share that vision with you now.

YOUR WORTH IS UNIQUE TO YOU

Some of our asks can use data to drive the "worth" meter. If you're negotiating salary and compensation packages for a new role, there is data out there that will give you a sense of what your role, at that level, in that industry, and in that location, is "worth." But even those data-driven salary ranges are not truly contextualized and specific to you, your circumstances, the conditions at the organization offering you a job, or the specific climate of your industry at the exact moment the offer is being made. The data create the equivalent of a ballpark, but not *your* ballpark. The data can be busted through and can't be the only thing that defines the target of your ask.

As for the bazillion other asks we make throughout our careers, there may be exactly zero available data to help us gauge the market. Are you going to pitch your book to your cousin's friend who's just starting to build her client list as a new literary agent? Or are you going to pitch to that agent you admire, who has the roster of authors you want to be associated with and can elevate your impact but feels out of your league? What data can you use to decide which of *those* two is the right ask? None. There is no clear and numerical data to guide you or shape your choice. You'll have to rely on other factors to make this call. Many asks we make aren't number-based, but they're just as potentially life changing as the ones that are.

When it comes to advocating for ourselves through a big ask, data can be a red herring. It makes us feel like we're basing our asks on some sort of objective reality, but that's just not true! No number of averages or percentages drawn from your industry's hiring activity can reflect what you, as an individual, can do when paired with the perfect company or given the perfect opportunity. Not to get all woo-woo on you, but your ask is actually about the synergy you'll create in partnership with an organization or person or role. No other person in the world will create that same synergy, which means that no predetermined salary range should hold you down. Data is great when you can get it, but it's not enough.

And even if you *have* data and a rough ballpark, you *still* might ask for and get less than what's possible, especially if you use your own evaluation of your worth without seeking outside input.

THE NUMBER IN YOUR HEAD IS ALWAYS TOO LOW

If you want to get a lightning bolt to the brain during one of my workshops, you can volunteer to have me live coach you in front of the room. Whenever someone does this, other participants assume we'll be shifting focus to that one person for a bit, but that's never the case. What ends up happening instead is the volunteer shares something that the whole room has experienced, and I tap the group's collective wisdom to help her puzzle it out. I invite them to coach the volunteer through her ask strategy using what we've learned in the workshop so far.

I remember one woman who raised her hand, looking panicked and thrilled all at the same time. She came to the front of the room and told us her story: She was a finance professional in her late twenties. Over the past few years, she'd gathered enough experience and chops to level up for the first major time after being hired right out of university. She was heading into negotiations with a new company for a new role, and was stuck on the question of salary. She kept trying to make herself answer "What number should I ask for?" but she was rattled. This was her chance to really bolster her income and claim her space in her career. She was determined to get paid what she's "worth." The hiring company really wanted her, and she could feel it. So we, in the workshop, asked her what number she had in mind. She took a breath and gave us a number. The room was nothing but crickets.

Our audience included one hundred women at various career levels and across multiple industries. When I asked, in the deafening silence, "Is that the right number?" the room blew up!

"NOOOO," they said, with equal parts conviction and love. "Go for more!"

Turns out, the number she gave us was what she thought she was "worth," but it was a good 30 percent lower than what the room thought was possible. And the room was full of women with more experience, more asks under their belts, and more objective perspective on this volunteer's marketability. In other words, this room of strangers had a wildly different—and arguably more accurate—idea of this young finance professional's true value in her role, in her industry, at this market moment in her career trajectory.

This is just one story, but the theme shows up over and over and over in my work.

If we ask for what *we* think we're worth, we often go too low. We forget that when we want to level up, we've got to reach higher than the rung we're standing on. Sometimes that means asking for quite a bit more than we think we're currently worth.

PRICE, VALUE, AND WORTH

Hopefully, it's becoming clear that our asks shouldn't be formulated around ideas of "worth." I have a hack that will untangle your "worth" from your ask, prepare you to ask for whatever the fuck you want, and position you to level up. And I'm almost there, I promise.

But first, a quick story about the difference between value and worth.

Remember those two auctions—the one with the art that sold for way less than the gallery thought it was worth and the glamping trip that sold for *way, way, way* more than the seller thought it was worth? Those auctions happened during the third year of my auctioneering adventures. They were two sizable auctions for two very different audiences and very different organizations but in the same-ish zip code. As a reminder, here's what happened: At one auction, I sold a piece of art that was supposed to be "worth" $10,000 for $4,600. At the other auction, I sold a one-night glamping trip worth no more than the street value of the reservation and the catering—around $20,000—for $55,000 . . . twice, back-to-back, to two different buyers. I was dumbstruck and fascinated in both of these cases. What were these items on the auction block truly "worth"? Fuck if anyone knows! That is, until you ask and find out what someone is willing to pay.

Just hold that in your heart for a sec.

When I'm preparing to run an auction, my fundraising clients will say, "We want to get $5,000 for this lot." (Remember, a "lot" is an item up for bid.) But here's the rub: I can't promise them I can get $5,000 for any given lot. I have absolutely no idea what it'll sell for. What am I gonna do? Yell at the audience, "Hey people! This freaking piece of art is 'worth' ten grand! Get your paddles in the air!" or "Hey y'all! What are you, nuts? This camping trip is worth twenty grand TOPS!" Nope. And that's because, and here it is folks,

Price is a measure of value, not a definition of worth.

I know this because I've seen it play out at auction and in our businesses and in our careers in a thousand colorful ways. We can do our best to set the stage by telling the story of the value of what we're selling (or asking for), but, ultimately, it's the room that decides. The room determines the price. (Though I have the power to say "yes" or "no" to that price if they want to negotiate.)

But let's get back to my client. When they tell me, "We want to get $5,000 for this lot," my answer is *always*, "I'll sell it for whatever anyone in the room will pay for it, as long as it's above our reserve." That way, we're safe on price. I'll never say "yes" to an offer from the room that is below our reserve, and the sky's the limit for anything above that. Well, to be more accurate, the highest bidder is the limit when it comes to what will become the selling price. I could never have predicted a fairly modest glamping trip would go for $55,000, nor could I have predicted that a covetable piece of art would go for less than half of what it was supposed to be "worth."

And when you enter your ZOFO to make an ask, you, too, can be dumbstruck and fascinated at the answers you get. This is the thing that can turn an ask that feels hard into an adventure. When you go to tackle your next big ask, here's how you can reframe the ideas of price, value, and worth. This will protect you from interpreting the answers you get as an ironclad definition of your worth and will free you up to challenge what you think is possible:

> **Price is a way for you to see what they (your audience) value, and not a way to define your worth(iness).**

Or, let me dice it up using the first version I showed you a few paragraphs ago:

> ~~Price~~ **What they'll do or pay is** ~~a measure of value~~ **a way to see what they value and how they value it,** ~~not your worth~~ *not* **a way to define or measure your worth(iness).**

You get to choose your reserve, and *you* get to interpret how folks perceived your ask through the lens of how they responded or what they offered or counteroffered. Once you have an answer or offer in hand, your job is to recognize that that answer is about them, not you.

You might be thinking, "Nice idea, dude, but aren't value and worth/worthiness kinda same-same?"

Not in my book. I mean, not in *this* book, but also, metaphorically, not in my book!

In this book and in my view, value is transactional. The amount exchanged in that transaction—the "this for that"—is an indication of how someone values something in comparison to something else. (A less or more expensive thing.) It's shopping.

Worth and worthiness are rooted in the self. They're your inherent enough-nesses that let you pursue your dreams. They're your humanity. They are *not* shopping.

Put that truth in your pocket and just carry it around with you.

INTERPRETING THE ANSWERS AND OFFERS YOU GET

"
Worth and worthiness are rooted in the self. They're your inherent enough-nesses that let you pursue your dreams.
"

I see it like this: You are worthy of any ask you make. You are worthy of your goals. The asks and transactions associated with those asks are a vehicle to get you to your goals, to build a life or business or career or community that aligns with your vision for yourself. That means you get to decide what you say "yes" to and who you say "no, thank you" to. The question isn't "What are you worth?" The question is, "Is what they've offered worth it to you?"

Now, I talk a lot about getting more, but "more" isn't reserved for easily quantifiable things like salary, project price, hourly rate, or being able to run that big-ass, high-visibility project. Sometimes your more can be a deeply personal and less yardstick-y type of more. Maybe your more is more of the right kind of client who falls outside your immediate network but is exciting and totally aligned with your new mission. Maybe your more is a bigger stage, or a book deal, or landing that one meeting that can change everything. Maybe your more is connecting with the right mentors who make you feel a little starstruck but have the power to change your trajectory. Maybe your more is doing more of what you love. Maybe your more is gaining total control over your time.

You're allowed to want whatever you want more of. And if you ask for what you want more of and get a counteroffer, only you can decide if that counteroffer is acceptable or too much of a compromise.

Let's use my career as an example. I've done some fancy-pants strategic engagements as a leadership communications coach. My job is to help high-impact leaders speak from the heart, with strategic storytelling in high-stakes moments. I've worked on campaigns that had billion-dollar decisions on the line and in high-level meetings where the globe's biggest challenges are addressed. You know, big shit that sounds fancy and exclusive. I've also, through my participation in and support of nonprofits and communities working on local initiatives, worked with founders where the stakes are high *for them and their organizations*, but the actual projects are on the least sexy topics you can possibly imagine and oftentimes look small by comparison.

These two categories of work do not yield the same coaching or speaking rates. They can't. Not by a long shot. So I've carved out a policy that says I'll do a certain number of engagements each year at a low-bono rate for organizations that are aligned with the mission at the heart of this book and other social impact I'd like to have with my work. This means sometimes, I am one price, and other times, I'm another. I am willing to go lower because the work is worth it to me. It satisfies something other than my pocketbook and my P&L. Underneath all these numbers are people and contexts and circumstances. In some cases, my commercial rates are where it's at; in other cases, my low-bono rate is right and is an absolute stretch for the organization. A stretch that is meaningful, chock-full of gratitude, and so undeniably on-mission for me that I'd do it for eighty-nine cents.

So, what am I worth? Big numbers? Small numbers? Eighty-nine cents? Who the fuck knows!

The question to ask instead is, "Is this work, at this rate, *worth it to me?*" I get to say. I get to decide. I hold the power, and the transaction isn't a definition of my worth. It's a choice I get to make based on what I know my audience will pay or can pay for what I'm offering. Your worth is infinite; any one transaction is contextual.

> "
> *Your worth is infinite;
> any one transaction is
> contextual.*
> "

And you, too, can use this question to gauge how folks value what you bring, get more of what you need, and hold onto your power. *You* get to decide what you'll say "yes" to.

Marcus said it best.

Marcus the Miraculous sat toward the back on a velvet event chair. He quietly listened to the ideas in our "Your Most Powerful Ask, LIVE!" workshop. (Yes, it was a mixed-gender room.) He took notes here and there and looked at the content. He was invited to this workshop as part of his company's initiative to support, develop, and advance Black and Latino marketers in their global organization. Marcus was what the room needed.

As we approached the section of the workshop where we address the idea in this chapter—that price is a measure of value, not worth—things got tense.

In the back, one executive sponsor of the program sharked around, picking off the buffet of snacks laid out on the well-decorated table. He squinted, raised his hand, and interrupted.

He wanted to debate semantics; he wanted to challenge the definition. He wanted a teardown in the most intellectual way. The air in the room changed.

Marcus the Miraculous stood up. He was enormous. Energetically and physically, he took up space. The room settled and locked in on him. In his gentle but firm voice, he stated, "No. Value is situational. You walk into one room, into one meeting as a designer, and your value is perceived at one level. Even before you speak, share an idea, or contribute. In another meeting your value is perceived differently. And you can see, easily, that in each of these situations your value is marked somewhere based on the folks in the room and the need in this situation. You will establish your value with them as you contribute, as you share your ideas and collaborate, and you can shift their notion of how they value your presence and your contribution. But it's always moving. Always changing.

"How folks perceive your value is contextual. That's them. That's what they see, assume, have exposure to. They have no idea what you're capable of, what you can do. But they peg a value based on their needs, perspective, and experience in that context. As you move from room to room, from context to context, you don't change, but how others value what you do does. Your salary? Your bonus? The projects you're given? All indications of what they value and how they value it. And even that is contextual.

"But that has absolutely nothing to do with your worth—nothing to do with your worthiness. Because your worth and worthiness are infinite."

Mic drop, Marcus, mic drop.

APPLYING THIS IDEA AND STRATEGY

Applying this idea is simple. You're staring at the ask. Ready to make it. Remember, the answer you get—yes, no, or negotiate—is not a way to measure your worth. Instead, you are using this as a way to see who the players are, what they value, and how they value it in this particular context. You then get to put that information up against what you value and see how those things align, or don't.

Don't ask, "What am I worth?"

Ask, "Is it worth it to me?"

Trina the Titan stepped out of her high-paying, high-powered marketing job with a big brand to start her own agency. Combined with this change, she moved to a new state and aspired to work in a new industry and market. Was she starting from scratch? Yes—and no. No, because she was a seasoned professional in marketing for CPG (consumer packaged goods) and for big brands. And yes, because she was moving cities, moving industries, and moving markets. It was a fresh start, but not a start from scratch. Only a month into her new business, she wrote a proposal for a four-month contract with a sizable brand. They couldn't meet her price, but she still wanted the gig because she was at the beginning of building her agency. Instead of simply saying "yes" when there actually wasn't enough of what she valued in their counteroffer for her, she took a step back and asked, *What if their budgets are constrained to this dollar amount—would that make this engagement worth it to me?* She knew it was imperative to be able to pay the bills. There was a minimum she needed to earn, and this counteroffer met that (barely), but paying the bills wasn't all she needed. Her goal was to build a reputable agency and to do that she needed to make rent but also needed to grow her leads list, her network, and her portfolio. She needed to use this opportunity to add something that had huge value to her and that she could leverage into a future benefit. So she had her answer and she countered their counter with additions like:

- *Be* the *point of contact for all PR engagements*, so she could build relationships and a reputation with PR agencies in the area and inside that industry.
- *Be a spokesperson for the organization at all strategic and industry-facing events*, versus being behind the scenes so she could build relationships with other possible clients.
- *Permission to create and publish case studies she could use in her business marketing*, so that she could establish credibility in this market.

Were those additions, those asks, ZOFO-ish? Yes. And did they say "yes"? Yep. Because she worked with what both they and she valued and did not let their offer hold her sense of worth hostage. Instead of taking the low offer as a sign of her worthiness, she found a way to balance what she needed and wanted with what they could do by not asking, "What am I worth?" but instead, "What would make this worth it to me?"

And she knew that if it wasn't worth it to her, *she* didn't have to say "yes."

CHAPTER 10

Your Market Is Bigger Than the Room

Idea: Your market is bigger than the room.

Strategy: Keep an abundance mindset to allow you to risk getting a no, knowing that there are other markets for your ask.

Every auction is a micro market. In the room, we have 50 or 100 or 250 or 1,000 people who make up the market at that moment. I know that I have bids to conduct, and we've prepared well, knowing our lot order, opening bids, and reserve for each and every item we'll put up for auction.

It doesn't happen often, but sometimes our reserve isn't met, and we pull the lot out of the auction right then and there and move on. We decide not to sell it because the people in the room don't want it at the reserve we've set. Fine. That's OK. We'll take that lot and save it for another audience, we'll put it up on the gallery wall and sell it at retail, we'll put it in the silent auction next year—we'll do something else. Because, while I'm auctioneering right here, right now, our market outside of this moment is bigger than that room.

So is yours.

In this book, I'm sharing ideas and strategies that may feel daring and status quo–challenging—because they are. They're simple and bold and for those critical moments along your path where asking big and knowing what *you'll* accept feels like a risk—because it is.

But it's a risk that's more possible to take when you use the idea that your market is bigger than the room.

Look, asking for more and risking a no isn't easy. When you're making a ZOFO-type ask, you do so knowing that you're not playing small, carving down your asks, or leaving money and opportunity on the table. Asking big and risking a no requires an abundance mindset. A mindset that acknowledges the renewable resource that is opportunity. You may feel like every big ask will make or break your future, but it won't. There will be other people, other opportunities, and other markets that will value your asks differently. An auction event may be confined to one room, one market, and one moment in time, but *your* market is much bigger. It's bigger than the room you're in, bigger than this one job interview, bigger than the single audience you're speaking to right now. There will be others. Trust that, and you will be able to take the perceived and sometimes real risk of making a ZOFO ask. Give yourself permission to walk away from an audience who's just not buying what you're selling at the rate you want to sell it, and save it for another day, another market, or another moment.

> " *Give yourself permission to walk away from an audience who's just not buying what you're selling.* "

Take this book, for example. The proposal alone was like sixty thousand pages of effort and thinking and then . . . I had to sell it. I pitched and queried. I knew the kind of publisher I wanted to work with and, wow, months of pitching to micro markets yielded zero results. I got some counteroffers, but nothing was right. But I knew my market was bigger than the room. I trusted this as I continued to take my ask to new markets until . . . well, I'm writing this book for you now with a publisher who is absolutely fabulous and right for this project.

Do not despair when the market you are asking in isn't responding the way you want. Lean on your reserve and know that your market is bigger than the room. I listed

> **"There will be other people, other opportunities, and other markets that will value your asks differently."**

above many of the other places we can find another market for the piece of art that won't sell for above our reserve tonight, but maybe will tomorrow somewhere else. Online auction, private showing, silent auction next year, other collectors we approach individually—the list could go on.

When we go into an auction, we know those other opportunities for selling exist. But you may not yet have a clear view of your other markets.

For your ask, your market may feel like a last-chance movement—like if you don't get what you're looking for this time, there will never be a next time. And last-chance thinking begets last-chance thinking. So look at the ask you're about to make of the market you're about to make it to (even if it's one person), and take a moment to do some of that abundance mindset shit everyone is talking about. You know, all that "the universe will provide" and "I have all I need" stuff. Turn to the coffee mug aisle in your local discount designer retailer for your favorite abundance mindset mantra. Browse the aisles, and, if that cow mug with the 3D udder design that says *Life is good. Milk it!* inspires you? So be it. If you prefer your inspiration to have a little more of a sober tone with a hint of cultural appropriation and influencer culture, maybe reach for, mentally, the mug that just simply says *Namaslay* in that oh-so-soothing pastel lettering. Great. Do you.

So you've got your mindset right. Let's do a visualization. Look forward into the future, picture all the other people, companies, teams, and organizations you'll talk to over the course of your life and over the course of getting this ask answered with what you need to move yourself forward. Picture all those super fun conversations you'll have where things just click, where the person you're talking to feels so familiar. Picture their faces looking so interested in your setup for the ask. Notice how it feels to be in conversation with the markets of your future. You're laughing and connecting; you have so many things in common. They *get* you. You are *Namaslay*ing.

Now look back, reflect on all those conversations and asks you had to make to get to where you are now. Remember how you felt super last-chance-y about one or two of those. And yet, the universe supplied you with new markets for the asks, applications, auditions, and connections you needed to get to where you are right now. You've done this before. You've *Namaslay*ed.

When I was a kid, we used to go across the street to Mrs. Alkamer's house. She lived in the only house on our block that had a huge lot (it was the original one-story farm house that came with the land that had been subdivided, post-World War II, into a solid, six-block square of single-family homes). Her driveway was long and only as wide as a single car and lined with a picket fence on one side and a rose garden on the other. We'd go there and, in the cool shade of the oak tree that covered nearly half her property, take rocks from her driveway. They were nice ones. And she let us do it. We'd pick a set of them—always the ones with a little quartz sparkle buried in the gray, dusty everyday-ness of a good old driveway rock. We'd take them home, wash them, polish them, and coat them with olive oil or Crisco or whatever we had that made them look wet and shiny. Then we'd display them on a beautiful doily spread over a small tea tray and walk them house to house selling them for five cents a rock. Our goal? Enough earnings to afford two candy bars from the corner store.

Our neighborhood had some flagship residents, but other homes had rotating renters, and you never knew who would come to the door. We'd knock on Johnny's door, and his aunt would answer and usually say no. But our market was bigger than the room, and we never knew which door would be a yes and which would be a no. Some would even negotiate.

"I'll give you seven cents for those two, final offer."

If we had only knocked on Johnny's door, we never would have earned what we needed for that Snickers and Charleston Chew (I liked the strawberry ones) we'd set out to buy. So we'd knock and knock and knock. Even Mrs. Alkamer would buy back her own rocks, but not consistently and not always for the same price.

Those three hours we'd spend selecting, polishing, and shopping our wares was a condensed version of what we do in our adult lives, businesses, and careers. While back then, we were looking

> " *Your market is bigger than the room. Bigger than this one moment.* "

to make a buck twenty in one sprint on a Saturday, in adulthood, we are looking to raise millions, elevate our roles, and bring to life projects over the course of years.

In those early days, each door was a micro market, and my market was bigger than each door. If I'd stopped at the first door, I'd never have enjoyed the delight of a strawberry Charleston Chew fresh out of an overnight in the freezer.

Your market is bigger than the room. Bigger than this one moment. Trust that, and you can take the risk knowing you've got options.

APPLYING THIS IDEA AND STRATEGY

Breathe. You will get a no. The kind that won't even reach your reserve. So, when that happens, DO NOT:

- Tell yourself your ask is stupid.
- Lower your reserve against your will.
- Abandon your dream.
- Find reasons why what you want is a problem and talk yourself out of wanting it.
- Give up before it's really time to change course.

- Get talked into believing you're too much.
- Get talked out of what matters to you.
- Be deterred.

DO:

- Take your offer off the table.
- Say "thank you for your time," snap-lock your power briefcase, and exit with confidence.
- Think "What would Beyoncé do?"—and do that.
- Remind yourself that your market is bigger than the room.
- Consider asking your audience who else may be good to turn to.
- Keep it classy.
- Look elsewhere.
- Keep *Namaslay*ing.

Just because you can't sell it now, doesn't mean you can't sell it. Your market is bigger than the room.

This case study draws on my own story.

This book, the one you are reading right now, needed to be sold. Like with our Mrs. Alkamer's rocks reselling scheme, I had preparations I needed to make in order to sell the manuscript. I had to develop these ideas in front of live audiences, figure out how to write a proposal, write the proposal, realize the proposal sucked, rewrite the proposal . . . and then it came time to send it out—to knock on doors. With my proposal spread out on a metaphorical doily, I went a-knockin'. In my first attempts, my first asks, I got rejected! Or in the language of this book, I stepped into my ZOFO and asked for more than I thought I could get and many times, found that it was indeed more than I could get. I got hard noes. And I got ghosted—I couldn't even get to the point of asking, "Are you in, or are you out?"

because the silence my asks were met with was clearly saying, "I'm out." But I drew on the idea in this chapter and persevered, whispering to myself, *Your market is bigger than this room.* Holding onto that idea let me continue to find new markets, new audiences, and new rooms, and soon? The ask I made was met with a yes. And here we are, chomping through a frozen strawberry Charleston Chew.

CHAPTER 11

Purpose Drives Courage

Idea: Purpose is a source of courage.

Strategy: Get clear on your purpose, and use that to fuel your courageous asks.

When I work with leaders to help them speak powerfully on stage, in a boardroom, in their organization, or at any moment when stakes are the highest, we can't fiddle around with scripts and what to say here or what to say there and whether standing here or there is better for the moment. We can't get into the weeds on where to place emphasis or how to craft a key message. We have to start with purpose.

When you're clear on purpose, you can speak more courageously. You'll know what to say and how to say it because it'll be tied to something greater—it'll be in service of something bigger. And, it makes it easier to have a higher impact in the front of the room because you can source some courage from your purpose. It's a wellspring.

We never start writing a script or crafting a message until we are clear on the purpose the upcoming communication or speech serves. From that we can draw on the courage we need to tell a compelling story—to rewrite the expected scripts and do something uniquely aligned to that leader's voice.

> **When you're clear on purpose, you can speak more courageously.**

When we remind ourselves of the purpose of this moment, we are drawn toward the more courageous choices, even if the courageous choice is a surprising one.

A note on courage: It's easy to think that courage comes packaged in extroversion, especially when it's tied to something in the vein of ambition. But no, often the courageous choice can be subtle. Some of my clients' courageous choices have been:

- Choosing simple and direct communication
- Choosing to share a personal story
- Acknowledging when they're lost along the path of doing something hard
- Sharing the stage with someone who intimidates them
- Taking a stage that intimidates them

All of these were courageous choices, and they were easy choices to make because these people were clear on their purpose in those moments.

A lot of what I describe in this book takes courage. I've given you tools that I hope will unblock you—get you over yourself enough to step into your ZOFO and go for more of what you want. But if your coals of courage are not burning hot enough, consider this: Purpose is a source of courage. Fall in love with your purpose and the goals embedded within it. When you use your purpose to guide your actions, you'll never lowball yourself again.

You are free to love your purpose more than you hate getting a rejection. You're free to ask for whatever you want and need to reach your goals. For you, your purpose for asking for a raise may be to afford piano lessons for your child because it's their newly discovered passion. The ask you're making may let you expand your business, providing employment and economic stability for families in your community. Or your ask might help you offer access to professional development to young women, or work to end prison recidivism, or travel the world on a sailboat. Only you can identify and decide the why behind your ask. But when you do that, a bigger ask becomes easier to make. Purpose will give you the courage you need to make the kinds of asks that get you more.

As an auctioneer, I often use purpose as my source of courage. I channel the mission statement of the organization for whom I'm raising money when I ask the audience for just a little bit more. I focus on that mission as I let that awkward silence stand for just a minute longer, seeing if one more donation will come in or

> **You are free to love your purpose more than you hate getting a rejection.**

if anyone else wants to beat my top-dollar ask. Sometimes the answer is yes, sometimes the answer is no. But no matter what, purpose gives me the courage to stand in my ZOFO, even when it scares the hell out of me. I remember *why* I'm there, and that gives me the courage to ask for more. And get it.

APPLYING THIS IDEA AND STRATEGY

When you get stuck, have a hard time stepping into your ZOFO, and need courage to act on an ask you need to make, turn to your purpose and see how it can be a source of courage. You can:

- Journal about the purpose that your ask is helping bring to life.
- Connect with a friend and have a conversation about your purpose so you can breathe life into it.
- Make a playlist with songs that speak to your purpose and listen to it when you need to summon courage.

Unrelated to asking, but totally related to using purpose as a source of courage, this case study is about someone who took a stage.

Years ago I had the opportunity to work with Dana the Determined, a leader and human rights activist. They were presenting at a global meeting where members of large governmental and nongovernmental agencies would be in the audience. They had been invited to receive an award for their lifetime achievements and to speak about their work. This was their moment to have a huge impact on an audience of people who hold the pens that write policy, have the ability to move resources, and can elevate the issues they care about. I was brought in to help ensure they were successful with their three minutes on stage.

In my communications work, I approach critical communications moments with the perspective and belief that when we speak from who we truly are, we are powerful. So when this leader shared with me how worried they were about the possibility that they would "show too much emotion" on stage during the acceptance speech and that they *also* wanted to have big impact on the audience, we were stuck. This leader, full of passion, still needed courage to speak from the heart in order to have their desired impact.

So where did we go? Purpose. Before looking at their script, before polishing and practicing, we spent time just storytelling—capturing their work, what mattered to them, and what they knew was their purpose. When we were finally ready to rehearse, we checked back in about how they were feeling.

They'd reawakened the courage to speak from the heart, to allow their most powerful and vulnerable voice to show up instead of spending time and effort squinting under their own light and hiding their emotions. Did they "overemote"? No. Did they show up in their full power with emotion? Yes. Did they have an impact on the entire audience? Yes.

They'd used their purpose as a source of courage.

That night, they brought the house down.

CHAPTER 12

Be an Agent for Your Purpose

Idea: Be an agent for your purpose.

Strategy: Act on behalf of your purpose in order to advocate for it with more freedom and less fear.

When I'm auctioning an item, I'm neither the buyer nor the seller. I'm an agent for the seller, and I work in their best interest. This is a powerful perspective that we can use to help us step into our ZOFO. It can make it feel easier to advocate for our purpose with more freedom and less fear. My ask isn't about me; it's about the entity I'm assisting, brokering, advocating for, and/or representing. When it isn't about me, I can empower my ask.

FROM SQUEEZED TO FREE

When I first started auctioneering, it felt scary. I wanted to perform well and keep track of my numbers, and I felt pressure to hold the steering wheel tightly, do my job, and get off the stage. Even though I was in my forties and someone who has spent thousands of hours in front of audiences big and small, auctioneering—even as an impact hobby—felt like a performance that was high stakes and all about me and my skills.

All about me—ego (and not the good kind).

I struggled to find a role in the conversation that would allow me to have a bigger impact and give me the freedom to tell stories in a way that connected with audiences before, during, and after the asks and negotiations I was conducting. I struggled to go beyond the transactional aspects of those moments. I struggled to access my creative self on stage and relate authentically with my audience. I wasn't having fun. And having fun—feeling alive and connected—is important even when it's the serious kind of fun. (Because what we are fundraising for is very often serious:

- breast cancer patients and survivors
- environmental stewardship
- artist-in-residence programs for veteran and parent artists
- access to open space for underserved communities
- job training and support for women
- equal representation in media
- arts education and career support for artists with developmental disabilities
- photojournalism for youth empowerment

Serious, important stuff.)

But then in the struggle to find my voice on stage as an auctioneer, I remembered that I, as an auctioneer, am not the buyer or the seller, but an agent.

An agent for what?

For the transaction and technically for the seller, yes. But, more importantly, I was the agent for the purpose that transaction was meant to support.

Once I clocked that—like, really internalized that—the gloves were off. That understanding gave me the space and the freedom to have the conversation with the audience that really needed to happen. It gave me the courage to talk up what needed to be talked up to provide a platform for the asks I was about to make. It let me tell my own story in relation to the purpose of the organization, making me *part of* what was happening, helping me connect with the audience about why we're here, together, in catalyzing change, together.

And you can harness this thinking too.

BE AN AGENT FOR YOUR PURPOSE

You have a purpose. Every ask you make is tied to something bigger than the ask itself.

You need a 10 percent raise *so that* you can finally buy your first house and your daughter can have her own room.

You're asking for that donation *so that* you can run a successful campaign and advocate for more equitable policy in accessing healthcare.

You're asking to attend that super exclusive leadership meeting *so that* you can advance your career along the path to becoming a director *so that* you can deploy agile methodology across all project teams *so that* you can ship that medical technology faster and save some lives already.

You're asking to renegotiate your full-time gig to a contract position for more money on the hourly rate *so that* you can start your own consulting company that will bring data intelligence to an industry woefully in need of it.

You're asking for that sabbatical *so that* you can live your dream of sailing around the world and make it possible for you to look back on your life and know that you did the thing you dreamed of.

What have you always fantasized about that feels out of reach

> "
> *Every ask you make is tied to something bigger than the ask itself.*
> "

but maybe isn't, because you can make a big courageous ask to fulfill your purpose?

It's so often easier to advocate for our purpose than for ourselves. So do it.

GIVE YOURSELF SOME DISTANCE

So many women I talk to share with me things like, "I have zero problem negotiating a multimillion-dollar deal for my organization. Why is it so hard to ask for things for myself?"

The truth is, I have no idea why it's so hard. At least, I have no idea why it's so hard for *you*. Why it's hard is unique to everyone.

But what I *do* know is that when you are an agent for your purpose, it can give you enough space to advocate for that purpose with more freedom and less fear.

BUT, HOW?

Let's make it concrete. The first thing to do is notice if the ask you are about to make is a ZOFO ask—the kind that threatens a no, the one that challenges what you think you can get, the one that has all the potential. If the answer is "yes"—that, my friends, is a ZOFO ask. Great. Now ask yourself if this ZOFO ask is one that is going to be so ZOFO-ish that the other ideas we've shared so far won't help you ask it—the ideas like:

- "Hey, remember, people are irrational, and sometimes their rationale isn't your rationale" and . . .
- "You got your reserve nailed down, and you know your boundary; plus, you've got a plan if they won't even say yes to that, so you got this" or . . .
- "What they'll say yes or no to is just a way to know what they value, not a way to define your worth," and even . . .

- "This won't be the last ask you'll make, and this isn't the only person in the world to ask—your market, dear one, is bigger than this room."

If these aren't the elixirs that will make it possible for you to step into that ZOFO, take the second step and ask yourself: "If I am an agent for my purpose, can I make this ask?"

Then reach for that purpose and activate it. Take a few moments to visualize the outcome you are trying to reach with this ZOFO ask. Imagine that your

> **" When you are an agent for your purpose, it can give you enough space to advocate for that purpose with more freedom and less fear. "**

purpose is outside of you—it has a life of its own but also can't come to its fullest potential without you. Like a child needing that supportive presence when taking their first steps, or like that younger you who needed an advocate, stand next to your purpose like you're doing it together.

Your role now is not to ask for yourself but to be that advocate, champion, and sponsor for your purpose. Be its agent and make the ask on behalf of that purpose you have now reconnected with.

Now, step three: Connect the ask and the purpose with a story. In this step we want to craft the story that connects the ask to the purpose it is helping to fulfill. We want to get this story straight for ourselves, because when we can tell the story for ourselves, it comes alive, makes more sense, and helps us access our courage. When it's clear *why* we're making that ZOFO ask, it's just easier to do it.

Here are a few frameworks to do that. You can pull out a pencil and Mad Libs them if you like. And if you are too young to know what Mad Libs is, well, thank goddess for the internet.

When I make this ask, I am advocating for [purpose] _____

_____.

My purpose is to [purpose] _____
and I am acting as its agent and ambassador when I ask for [ask] _____
_____.

When someone says yes to [ask] _____, I
am helping to make possible [purpose] _____
_____.

For me, when I am prepping to auctioneer, this can sound like:

When I make this ask, I am advocating for *making it possible for women facing breast cancer treatment to get their utility bill covered for six months.*

And in our everyday lives it might sound like:

My purpose is to *help one million women ask for more and get it and put more money and decision-making power in their hands*, and I am acting as its agent and ambassador when I ask *to partner with this organization*.

When someone says yes to *this contract at this rate*, I am helping to make possible *financial security for my family*.

Once we've connected our ask and our purpose, we can use that story to fuel our courage and share that story with our audience in the setup for the ask.

APPLYING THIS IDEA AND STRATEGY

Have an ask that feels too ZOFO-ish?
   Remember:

1. Purpose is a source of courage.
2. Be an agent for your purpose.

3. Do that by:
    i.   Evaluating whether the ZOFO ask needs a purpose boost to help you make it.
    ii. Visualizing and reconnecting to the purpose your ask is serving.
    iii. Linking the ask and the purpose with a story.

Jade the Champion needed to find a way to make her nonprofit more sustainable.

Her idea was to pursue corporate sponsorships to fund the programs in her nonprofit. She was set to pitch her first potential corporate sponsor and called me. In our call, we talked about her ask, made sure it was big enough to threaten a "no," and got clear on her reserve. When it was time to wrap the call, she said, "I don't know why, but asking for others is so much easier than asking for myself." I pointed out that she wasn't asking for herself; she was asking for her organization, the one she founded with a very specific social impact purpose. When I offered her the idea of being an agent for the purpose of her organization, her mindset shift changed everything. She went into the ask with a confidence and clarity she didn't have before.

When we are an agent for our purpose—when we are fighting for "it," rather than ourselves—we can create just enough space to advocate without personalizing the ask or the response we get.

CHAPTER 13

Inside Every Ask Is an Offer

Idea: Inside every ask is an offer.
Strategy: Find that offer to sell your ask for the highest bid.

A decade ago I participated in one of those professional development experiences where you, you know, learn stuff about yourself. In this case, it was a one-day immersive experience to see, name, and claim who you are when you are at your most compelling. *Gulp.*

In this case, we were given a challenge to go around town and get something like "a coffee for free at a coffee shop" or a tour of the kitchen of someone's restaurant. Or for someone to give us their socks. And the challenge was to get these things "as your most compelling self—fully in your archetype"— to take what we'd discovered about ourselves (a sort of archetype) during the in-class exercise, and be *in* that archetype while we executed the challenge.

The challenge I took on was to get someone to give me twenty dollars. A twenty-dollar bill. A twenty. Twenty bucks. A twamp. A Jackson. A dub. Or, if things work out, a Tub, since Harriet Tubman is slated to replace Jackson on the twenty-dollar bill. Let's go!

It's kinda on-brand for me to ask for cashola. And this was a decade before auctioneering school!

And so out into the world we went, me and a partner.

After wandering around the tiny seaside town where the event was happening, we soon identified our audience. A group of white-sock wearing, middle-aged golf dudes. They walked in our direction as a small group, with hands on their guts, laughing a bit and, we could tell, sharing stories about their triumphs and losses and private equity deals and such. They were on a golf trip. Wives back at the resort, they were in town for breakfast before their tee time.

"Hey there!" I raised my voice and my cab-hailing hand to indicate I wanted to chat, and they walked over to meet us.

We chatted a bit, and I asked them where they were from, how they liked the fog, and if it impacted their game. I asked about the *really* nice resort they were staying at. I told a joke. We were having a nice time. Then, I just went for it.

"Hey, so . . . can I have twenty bucks?" I held out my hand and picked one of the men in the group and made eye contact. *Yeah, I'm looking at you.*

He was the oldest guy in the group. Clearly the alpha, the godfather, of their golf family. He was physically the biggest, with the most robust voice and tone. He was playful and jolly and I could tell he liked to be the boss—choosing the restaurant, sitting at the head of the table, ordering for the group, leading the dinner conversation with his stories. You know the type. Maybe you are the type.

I could see him suck in his breath, place his hand on his wallet pocket, and then hesitate.

"Are you serious?" he asked.

"As a heart attack," I said as I held out my hand.

I could see him struggling. My ask had put him on the spot. My ask had put some pressure on our relationship—our brief but real relationship and the rapport I'd established in just two minutes. But they weren't enough—the relationship and rapport.

He took out his wallet and put it back. Shifted his weight from one foot to another. He needed a reason to say yes or say no. He liked me, I could tell, and he was intrigued and didn't want to say no, but he was unsure as to why he'd say yes.

So I made him an offer. One that made him feel seen. One that was all about what mattered to him.

"It'll be great," I said. "I'll get my twenty bucks as part of a challenge I accepted. And you? You'll be buying a great story about how some lady, a complete stranger, came up to you, asked you for twenty bucks, and you gave it to her. Just like that. No questions asked. Kind of a boss move. Don't you think? You'll have the best story at dinner tonight and it'll only cost you one Jackson. Imagine starting cocktail hour with 'You'll never guess what happened today . . .'"

I held out my hand again. Unwavering.

He let out a breath and smiled big. Like a light had gone off for him. He was tickled at the whole possibility of it all. He was delighted at what he was about to do.

He brought his alligator-skinned wallet around the front of his belly, slid his forefinger and thumb into the sleeve and pulled out a twenty from the thick pad of neatly pressed Jacksons. He slapped that greenback into my hand and said, joyfully, "Deal!"

With a laugh that sounded like *Can you believe I just did that?!* and his friends patting him on his shoulders, he sauntered away with his buddies, shaking his head and happy to have had the exchange.

I offered him a great story to enliven his tired repertoire. One that he could milk for weeks. One that would make him the life of the party. That's what he got.

And me? I got my dub. There is an offer inside of every ask. Find it.

YOUR OFFER INSIDE YOUR ASK

In my early days as an auctioneer, one of my mentors always said, "Our job is to lower the value of money in the room." In other words, when someone is *getting* something bigger, more important, and more meaningful than what

> **" There is an offer inside of every ask. Find it. "**

they're *giving*, they're more likely to give more.

My version of this wisdom is: inside every ask is an offer. When I stand on stage and ask my audience for a direct pledge of $1,000, for example, I am offering them the opportunity to live in alignment with their values. I'm offering them the chance to be part of a collective giving moment, and that is powerful. My audiences in fundraising auctioneering are there because they want to be part of something greater than themselves; they want to be seen and celebrated as generous. They want to know they are acting on their values. They want to impact something that matters to them. I'm the conduit that allows them to do that.

You can use this idea that inside every ask is an offer to find the intersection of *your ask* and *their desire/need*. This isn't manipulation; it's your job. And there are hundreds of ways my clients (and you) have asked for advice on doing this. Some of them may be familiar to you. Questions like, "How do I become a better storyteller to convince my stakeholders that a specific strategic decision is right for this project?" or "How do I get better at influencing people?" or "How do I pitch this?" and "How do I explain this to my boss so they'll go for it?" People have asked me how to sell their ideas in a million different ways. Now, I'm telling you: If you're going to sell your ask and get the highest bid—if you are going to support your ZOFO ask—find the offer you're making that's hidden inside your ask, and make it clear to your buyer what that offer is. And then sing it loudly in your lead-up to the ask.

GET TO THE HEART OF IT

You might feel intimated by this idea. *How would I even know what to offer? How do I think about what kinds of offers to make? Do I have to gift wrap it?*

First of all, get out of your head. You don't have to invent something new and fancy or poetic or something that is *way* better than the ask you're making. It's not a big, creative, gift-giving exercise. You don't need to be extravagant. And don't think of it as a tit-for-tat, *fine-I'll-take-this-if-you-take-that* kind of exchange. You're not trading Pokémon cards. We need to start with a disposition of generosity and with a genuine interest in helping someone be successful with what matters to them. We have to know what our big ZOFO ask is and then put it aside and look—really look—at the desires, dreams, goals, and values of the people we will bring our ZOFO ask to.

The people we ask for things often have desires like:

- To feel accepted and like they belong
- To be appreciated
- To satiate their curiosity and hunger for knowledge
- To strike back
- To be honored by their leadership and social group
- To live up to their ideals around social justice
- To be autonomous and independent, as well as unique and self-reliant
- To have power and influence to own one's will
- To form connections and relationships
- To accumulate something
- To gain social status and social significance
- To feel a sense of security

They have dreams like:

- Building a billion-dollar company while solving climate change
- Jumping ship and freelancing

Goals like:

- Meeting Jon Bon Jovi (Wow, I'm old.)
- Standing on a big stage one day
- Serving on a board for a high-profile nonprofit organization
- Becoming a people manager

Values like:

- Adventure
- Exploration
- Selflessness
- Citizenship
- Fairness
- Fun
- Optimism
- Success

Think of someone in your crew, community, workplace, or friendship circle. Really look at them, and examine what you understand about them. Maybe they're super curious and motivated by their insatiable hunger for knowledge (desire) and love to be the one in the room known for understanding something or being smart (desire). You know that they are working on a huge research project that will put their name on the map as *the* leading expert in their field (dream) and on securing a cohort of influential business leaders (one that will not include Jon Bon Jovi) to convene around the topic of that research to create a standards body that they will manage (goal). One of their hobbies is cave diving (probably an adventure or exploration value in there), and they love being in the mix with high-level leaders and household names (Maybe a success value in there?). When they speak, they speak about possibilities—they are an *imagine what we could do* kind of person (optimism and self-determination values could be lighting up here).

Even looking at people from afar, you may be able to gather a lot about them from reading their work, listening to their talks, asking others about them, noticing what events they go to, and observing who they know, and therefore assemble a pretty nice, generous, and maybe even accurate take on what they're all about.

This is the beginning of putting together an offer inside your ask.

In my case, in a fundraising auction, I haven't shaken hands with anyone in the audience. Never met them. Didn't sleuth the internet to read up on their backgrounds. Don't even know their names. But here's what I do know: They've come to an art auction event in support of an arts education nonprofit. So they probably like art and value the arts, education, and being engaged with community projects. Plus, they're probably a fan of this specific organization. They've already spent seventy-five dollars for a ticket to the event, so they're willing to hand over some money in support of this cause.

They are givers. Otherwise, they would not even be here.

They might also be collectors. Folks who curate their own collection to enjoy and share with others. They see themselves as having taste and/or knowing art. Everyone at the show looks amazing—high style and edgy. This crowd loves to be seen.

Maybe I don't have a full grasp of it all—their desires, dreams, goals, and values—but I've got a picture. I can piece together who these folks are and what motivates them, and I can do it with empathy, curiosity, and generosity. Then I can shape an offer in the room that resonates with that audience. And when I say "resonate," I mean motivate. Resonate in order to motivate.

"Tonight is a night when you just may find that one piece to complete your collection, or start your collection" is an offer that links our time together with what *they'll* get, gives them recognition of their "collector" status, and allows new collectors (or people too shy to say they're collectors but who want to say that they are) to see themselves that way too. To invite them into the community. To offer them the chance to belong. So when I make the ask for the dollar bills to buy a piece, the value they're getting from making a bid and winning isn't just the piece they'll purchase, but a chance to enhance something (their existing collection) or become something (a collector).

Or the offer might take shape a different way: "When you bid tonight, you are saying 'Yes!'" said in my gala gown with my finger pointed toward the ceiling at the exact crescendo of a dramatic *yes!*, "to what this organization stands for and works toward. You are acting on what you value and you are demonstrating to yourself, the world, and this community that you are *IN!* And, importantly, *you* are making possible the promise of this organization to (insert organizational impact here)."

You might be noticing that this is more positioning than pitching. And you're right. You're positioning the ask you are about to make as one that is connecting what matters to your audience and what matters to the mission, goal, or impact your ask will have.

You're not saying, "Give me this thing I'm asking for." But you're telling the audience that, in saying yes to this big ZOFO ask, they're giving you the money or time or connection or stage or mentoring or whatever, in exchange for the impact that it will have and how it aligns with what matters to them.

Know that it is more powerful to tap into the deeper needs of your audience than the surface stuff.

My encounter on the street with my twenty-dollar ask required I understood what my "client" was really getting. He was getting a story. But that story was an asset that let me offer him what he really wanted—to be the center of attention when he shared that story. And *that* is the offer he couldn't refuse.

Yes, your ask-ee may want a 20 percent return on their investment, but the want that may push them to a yes is the reputation that comes with being a winning early investor. They stand to gain the social cred that comes with being first and having it work out.

See? There's a difference between what they get and what they *really* get. Consider both when you are looking for the offer inside of your ask.

THE THREE TIERS OF OFFERS

In my fundraising auctioneering situations, the setup that ties my ask to what matters to the audience is usually around social impact, giving, and philanthropy, or a cause that is personal to those in the room. When I do a fundraiser for financial support for single moms who are going through breast cancer treatment, there are very often breast cancer survivors in the room.

So my work is tied to something different than how you might be using this book. You may be using it to advance your career, or a goal you have inside your current job, or your small business, or your startup as it moves into seed round fundraising.

So let's jump into your world. I've conducted, as I look back, nearly 9,453 coaching sessions across my communications work in workshops, private and small group cohort sessions, events, Olympic bidding campaigns, and nearly every context you can think of. I have noticed three tiers of needs you can address in your offer: personal, professional, and purpose-driven. Use them to look around for how to find an offer in your ask.

Tier One: Personal

Personal needs are all about what *they* get.

This is where the *what they get* is super concrete—something that is about giving them something they want for themselves. Think, access to Jon Bon Jovi. "When you say yes to this, you get to meet Jon Bon Jovi." It's a personal thing and doesn't advance anything tied to business or something external to their desires and experiences (as far as you can tell), but you know it's something that matters to them.

Or, "Help me with [insert ask] and I can get you into this event where everyone is in a ball gown, and I know how much you *love* to dress up."

Personal offers are about what they get.

Tier Two: Professional

Professional needs are all about what their *career, business*, or *goals* get.

To speak to these needs, position your ask as something that will help advance their career, business, or greater external goal. It's not about them; it's about what they are trying to do or make happen.

For example, "I know you're working on x in your career or trying to build y in your business or want to move forward with z goal. I know I'm asking for a connection to your [insert some important ZOFO-ish person]. This may give you a chance to start a conversation with the person in a way that may help you [insert thing]. And I would be so happy to endorse your [insert thing]."

In this way, your ask isn't extractive, but a legit pathway for your ask-ee to build a relationship with someone. You're illuminating a possible way you can work together and both get your needs met in a way that's tied to your individual goals, which are different but can leverage the same moment.

Tier Three: Purpose

Needs tied to purpose are all about what their *purpose* gets.

An example is, "Sarah, I know how much of an advocate you are for founders who are struggling to level up. As an executive in the startup space, I've seen you underwrite, sponsor, advocate for, and elevate first-time founders across tech functions for years, helping them be successful. You are a true champion. Last year we ran our pilot for our learning platform specifically for founders with the profile you work with. We want to make world-class expert content available to founders everywhere across industries—the exact folks in your network. I'm looking for two things: an opportunity to partner with your organization to bring this platform to [insert ZOFO audience size] and an introduction to [insert name of influential person who is a ZOFO-ish name for you]. When you help bring this learning to founders in your network you're doing what you always do, and I'm thrilled to have the chance to help you advance your mission and lead with your purpose of accelerating the next generation of founders globally."

Mic drop. Or, pause while you wait breathlessly and squarely in your ZOFO. Purpose-oriented asks are about what their purpose gets.

Frame It Up

You might be asking, "Yeah, but how do I enter the conversation?" I know, I know. Sometimes you don't have all the information you need. So here are a few ways to get into the conversation that let you make the offer inside your ask:

- **Make an observation.** This approach is rooted in what you see and perceive. "I see you attending all these networking sessions where I've heard you talk about the importance of community . . ." and then set up how your ask is aligned to that or will advance whatever they're working on tied to community.
- **Make a declaration.** This approach is rooted in what you know. "Generosity is at the heart of everything your organization does . . ." and then set up how your ask is aligned to that or will advance whatever they're working on tied to generosity.
- **Make a conversation.** This approach is rooted in asking questions to identify what matters. "I'm curious what you are working on right now . . ." and then set up how your ask is aligned to that or will advance whatever they're working on right now.

Warning! Warning! Warning! This is not about manipulation. This is not extractive. This comes from a place of authenticity and generosity. You should (and I don't use the word *should* often or lightly) delight in seeing someone get what you're offering. You *must* give yourself a sniff test and make sure that you aren't dealing in dishonesty and manipulation but instead bringing an honest approach to setting up the offers you're making inside your asks.

Now that we've got that straight, you're ready to get down to business and build a rock-solid ask plan.

APPLYING THIS IDEA AND STRATEGY

You're going to craft an ask. Before you make that ask, STOP! Spend a few minutes articulating what the offer is inside your ask. The offer can range

> **Delight in seeing someone get what you're offering.**

from something simple and ephemeral like "the great feeling you'll get from helping me achieve my goal!" to something more concrete like "a kick-ass marketing strategy" (you know, the thing they're buying) to something more nuanced like "your core identity as a group of philanthropists." Know what it is your audience wants and needs, and embed the method for achieving those goals in your ask.

And notice: When you know what the offer is inside your ask, how does that make it easier to make that ask?

JayJay the Generous was on a tear. She wanted to dig into her professional development and had dreams to be a manager soon. But she knew she needed something more so that she would have more than the title—she'd have the skills to be a good manager.

Part of her plan was to gain those skills through a manager development program she'd found outside of her company. Oh, she wanted it bad! It looked so good, the curriculum was on-point, she knew she'd learn so much from other participants in the program, and she was excited to gain this new skill set. One problem: it was expensive. She'd have to ask her manager for a budget, and her manager would probably have to go find it somewhere. Her manager would have to advocate for her in ways that, let's just say, she'd not seen before and didn't trust would happen.

But JayJay the Generous could not be deterred. So together, in our workshop, we poked around until we found the offer inside her ask. While she loved the idea of managing people and had been doing it on her own for years, she knew that managing people was not her manager's favorite thing—especially the *people* managing part of people managing. JayJay had been picking up the slack for years because her teams had been led by fairly weak managers and everyone would come to her instead for all the people manager-y things.

So she figured out that if she could get this hardcore, totally awesome, deep management development program under her belt, she'd be better equipped, more skilled, and more confident at helping support the team and even at managing in a peer-to-peer way until it was time to chase a manager role she could sink her teeth into.

What did that mean for her ask? It meant that inside her ask for considerable budget and time for the development program was an offer to support her manager more directly in supporting their team. And that was one thing her manger could advocate for.

Wrapping her offer in her ask, she was ready to take that thing to her manager. Once she had that offer in mind—something she had a strong hunch would be a motivating factor in her manager advocating for the budget and time she needed—she was unstuck and her ask was empowered enough for her to make it. And that matters. As the saying goes, you get none of what you don't ask for.

And if you can ask like an auctioneer, you'll at least make the ask and improve your odds of getting what you need—and maybe more.

PART III

Your Big Ask Plan

CHAPTER 14

Your Ask Is the Start of the Conversation, Not the End

L et's think back to where we started: *You will be too much for some people. Those are not your people.*

Feel that? With that in mind, I'm gonna say stuff about holding on and letting go. Hold on to the idea that your ask is the beginning of a conversation, not the end. Let go of the idea that if they ghost you or won't play ball with you, you did something wrong, so shame on you.

I know that sometimes it can feel like asking for too much will leave you with nothing at all. That's the risk of challenging what we think is possible. And I'm not naïve. Sometimes—*sometimes*—a big reach can bring the whole show to a screeching halt. Let's take a look at that.

> **You will be too much for some people. Those are not your people.**

There's a feeling that comes with getting ghosted—you've built rapport, you've set up the story, made the ask, and then nothing. The whole thing evaporates. There's a feeling that comes with experiencing someone just shutting down a conversation before it's had a chance to come alive. There's a feeling that comes with working with someone who isn't interested in engaging in an exchange to explore how we might find something that works. There's a feeling that comes with getting stonewalled before you can explore or know you've been heard. What do you call that feeling? I call it *gross*. It's just a gross feeling. And I've felt it. Last year I was on a call with a client, and they were so *into* the work we could do together for their upcoming leadership summit. I mean they were really into it. They asked me for a contract and they wanted to move forward fast. Oh man, this was gonna be good.

So I crafted the proposal based on what we discussed and shot it off. Nothing. For days. I was like *Hello*?

You might be wondering if it was a ZOFO-ish ask with a ZOFO-ish number on it. Damn right it was. We were aligned, they were ready to hear my number, and I was ready to negotiate because we, our relationship, seemed to be ready for negotiation. Nope.

Days later, I got a short, curt email that said, "Thanks for reaching out, but we don't have the budget, and we'll reach out sometime."

Ummm. OK. *But I thought you were so into this!*

They were not. And because they truncated the conversation, did a 180, and semi-ghosted me, I read them as not collaborative, not ready, not great, and not my people. In the first twenty seconds after reading their response, I had that feeling of *Shit! I broke it!* and then it quickly shifted to *Wait, if this is how they roll, they'd be difficult to work with*, and then that flipped to *I will be too much for some people. Those are not my people.*

So, actually, I had a close call. A real squeaker. Whew! Onward.

We have to avoid spending all our time, spirit, and energy on what reaction *not* to get. If we focus too much on avoiding rejection, we may not have the chance to pressure test our relationships, clients, managers, or circumstances in ways that are revealing and allow us to understand where others stand and, just as importantly, where we stand.

If you are hit with silence and your audience isn't responsive, great! Instead of moping, get back to work because your market is bigger than the room and someone else out there wants what you're selling! I can't stand on stage all day begging for bidders, and neither can you. Make the ask, see what happens, and stop using *they might not talk to me again* as an excuse to play small and *they might not go for it* as an excuse to ask for less. If you want to ask for more and get it, you have to ask for more and know you might not always get it.

So, we're gonna let go of the idea that if they ghost you or won't play ball with you, you did something wrong, so shame on you. Instead, we take the stance that every ZOFO ask can be the beginning of a conversation.

In auctioneering we do start at a low number. We open the bidding at $1 or $200 or $600 or whatever, and then we have a conversation that moves the bidding up and up until we sell the lot. I'm having a conversation with the room. I am telling a story and they are raising

> *If you want to ask for more and get it, you have to ask for more and know you might not always get it.*

their paddles and bidding and laughing and giving me small signals and winking at their friends and talking with their tables about this and that and I'm calling out the next number. It's a collaboration until we find where their needs and mine intersect, represented by a selling price.

And you can conduct these kinds of conversations too. But instead of starting low and going high, you'll start high, and work your increments downward until you land somewhere that is the perfect equilibrium (represented by the agreement you make together) that brings together what you're asking for and what they'll say yes to.

Just look back at all the times you've asked for something and it didn't in fact kill the conversation. Remember all those times.

You asked for a title and a team that was totally in your ZOFO. You got a *no, not that* and spent the next few months planning, together with your manager, a pathway to getting a *yes, for right now* for taking on a title and a team a little smaller than your original ask but above your reserve.

You asked your coach if you could be the lead-off batter on the team and she said, "No, not this time," but she moved you up in the lineup and collaborated with you on performance goals to get you to that lead-off position over time.

You asked for that hourly rate (full-on fucking ZOFO number) from your client and she said, "Good for you but our business can't afford that right now," and "Could we do an [almost-that] number now, and if in three months we're somewhere different, we'll renegotiate."

Or that time you asked to be the MC of your all-company offsite (super ZOFO but critical for the strategy of elevating your visibility to help you reach another goal) and your CEO said, "No, not that, but would you be willing to design and MC the product track, which is holding a hackathon the three days leading up to the all hands kickoff?"

BOOM!

THE BOOMERANG EFFECT

Ya just never know when they might come back. So while you will be too much for some people, and they are not your people, you also need to leave room for change. Why? Because the boomerang effect is real. The boomerang effect is when folks ghost you . . . and then come back to you. It's that thing that happens when people spin off because the deal couldn't go through or you needed to say, "No, thank you," and you went your separate ways. But then, something changes and they come back.

So we're not rage quitting when they ghost or won't chat or can't meet our reserve right away. We're not storming out all disrespected and mad about it. We're seeing that they're not picking up what we're putting down, and we're moving on. We're respectfully stepping away.

But we *are* taking notes. We're taking notes so we know for ourselves *no, thank you and not in a million years would I work with, for, or around you* or *hmm, that was weird; they just disappeared. Not sure what happened on that one, but if they come on back, I'd be open to talking,* or *so sad they couldn't find the budget and I'm not lowering my rates below my reserve, so hope they come back with a wad of cash cuz I like them!*

When we know if we feel like it'd be a *no way, I'm open to talking,* or *hellz yes* if they do boomerang back, we know where we stand.

And because we just respectfully exited stage right and didn't rage quit, when they do boomerang, we're not patching up some fiery crash of a relationship.

Does this mean we're not setting boundaries or are pretending something was OK when it wasn't? Nope. It means we are recognizing that boomerangs happen—we expect them, and we don't burn bridges unnecessarily.

Lead with empathy and generosity *and* boundaries. Because you never know when things might change.

The ask is the beginning of the conversation, not the end. And if your ask kills the deal, you were too much for them, and they are not your people, at least right now.

> **And if your ask kills the deal, you were too much for them, and they are not your people, at least right now.**

IT'S JOURNAL TIME! (Not the journaling type? Then just reflect—while you're waiting for the light to turn green, relaxing on a blanket at the park, raking the yard, or strolling to your friend's house to borrow a stick of butter.)

Have you experienced the boomerang effect? It happens. And keeping the door open for it to happen is key.

Use the prompts below to notice when you've experienced it:

- When in your life has something looked like it was gone, but it wasn't? (Pssst, think of something good.)

- When it came back, can you take some guesses as to why it did?
- What was your role in making it possible for it to come back?

Remember: Disappointment exists, and so do boomerangs.

CHAPTER 15

Confidence Is the Result of Action, Not a Prerequisite

I love confidence. And I don't have it as often as I like. Maybe this feels familiar to you. Let's talk about how to get it.

Chicken and egg.

Stuck between a rock and a hard place.

At sixes and sevens.

In the grip.

Stuck in a rut.

On ice.

All of these phrases have in common the idea of stasis—something needs to happen before something else can happen.

I need cash for a car, but I need a car to get to work.

I need a SAG (Screen Actors Guild) card to act professionally, but I need to do some acting to get a SAG card.

I need experience to get that first job, but I need that first job to get experience.

Something's gotta give to break the logjam. One of my old mentors used to say that when faced with these circumstances, someone has to take the bigger risk. In these *I need a big break* moments, someone has to leap, step, or even tiptoe into unknown territory to get the flywheel effect going.

An employer has to take a chance on you so you can break in.

You've got to take the risk of asking your new BFF if you can use her car four days a week for a month so you can get to work and make that moolah. (It's a risk cuz you're trusting your relationship is ready for that kind of sharing economy.)

That singer needs to accept the invitation to step on that stage to finally *be* a singer—to break through the barrier of only singing for her childhood stuffies.

Something's gotta happen.

> ## *Confidence is self-belief and self-trust.*

The same thing is true about confidence.

Before we dig in, let's define confidence. Confidence is self-belief and self-trust. We feel confident in our estimation (read: we trust our guess). I'm confident in my plan (read: I trust this plan). I'm confident in myself (read: I trust myself). Having confidence doesn't have to be the same as being fearless, and it isn't only present in the absence of nerves, doubts, or some anxiety around one situation or another. When we say someone is confident, we are guessing, based on behaviors, that they trust themselves and that they are self-assured. But we can't be totally sure how they're feeling. In my work in communications, I've collaborated with people at every level and in every sector. I've teamed up with people who are world-class and prize-winning leaders and innovators who look and seem confident, but behind closed doors, they share their fears, nerves, and anxieties about high stakes communications moments they must engage with to further their goals and fulfill their stated mission. Government officials, CEOs, top-tier technologists, authors, Olympians, entrepreneurs, you name it—many of these people seem confident because of how they behave. Oftentimes they do have trust and belief in themselves because their actions have built that self-trust and belief, but they also suffer from fear, nerves, and anxiousness when stakes are high. Just like you and me.

I know you want confidence, and you can get it, but you don't *need* it in order to act. Instead, you need preparation. Every one of my most high-profile clients spends more time on preparation than they do on building confidence.

ACTION IS THE CONFIDENCE FACTORY

I've offered you a bunch of ideas you can use as strategies to help empower your ask so you can make it in your ZOFO. But I also understand that when the chips are down, you want confidence to actually do the thing. I do too. The problem is that confidence is an outcome of action, not a prerequisite. So we have to act and expect confidence will follow.

Here's the deal: You can take action even when you aren't brimming with confidence. Action is the way you produce confidence. Acting is your confidence factory. One note: Don't expect the ZOFO to evaporate in the face of your accumulated confi-

> " *Confidence is an outcome of action, not a prerequisite. So we have to act and expect confidence will follow.* "

dence. The ZOFO is ever present. Your ZOFO is with you forever. Why? Because your ZOFO moves away from you. You run toward it, and it moves. It's always expanding, always evolving right along with you. Just look back. What used to feel like a big-deal ask, a ZOFO ask, now feels like table stakes. I can look back and remember a time when raising my rates to half of what they are today felt like jumping out of a plane with an untested parachute. I wasn't really sure how it was gonna work out and there was a chance I could actually fail, but . . . maybe not? *Not sure; just gonna jump.*

I look back now and see that it was marbles. Because, like the horizon, the ZOFO is a vast space always in the distance and relative to where you are now. It draws you forward. You'll always have one, so make friends with it.

I share this with you because the illusion that *if I just get enough confidence, I'll annihilate the ZOFO, and the damn thing won't be a problem anymore* is just that—an illusion. It doesn't work that way. Confidence does not kill all devils. The most successful, influential, trailblazing women I have had the privilege of working with over the years still have a ZOFO. It just looks different than it did five years ago or twenty-five years ago. They've not figured out how to crush it; they've figured out how to act in it without demanding from themselves perfect, shiny confidence. They've figured out that confidence is not a requirement for action but rather that confidence comes with action.

If confidence is a blocker for you—if it is *the thing* you think you need *before* you can act, you've got a hostage situation on your hands. I call this the Confidence Trap.

The need for confidence traps action, limiting us even further because action is the key to confidence. It's a hella chicken-and-egg situation. Super rock and big ole hard place. Very logjam. Let's break through that.

The first time I stood on stage with a mic in my hand, I was scared. But I looked out into that crowd of several hundred people and had no choice but to jump in. I could wait no longer, could gather no more confidence than the tiny seed I had (which was really more adrenaline than confidence)—I just had to start. Only afterward did I feel the confidence I so desperately wanted to feel beforehand. *Holy shit! I just did that! I can do this!*

I recognize this as a cycle that's true for many, many people. It's not just my experience, but one shared by thousands of my coaching clients. Let's take the story of Janet, a woman in the first communications workshop I ever gave. It was a presentation skills workshop, and Janet was afraid to present in front of the room. Afraid enough to tell herself and everyone else that she's "not good at this" because it felt so scary she couldn't even imagine presenting to a room without the color draining from her face. She was sure she would fail. She told us over and over, "I'm not good at this. If I were just more confident, I could do it. I need confidence, and then I'll step up and present to the room." She was looking for information, tactics, and that one silver bullet that would make it possible for her to *finally* raise her hand and say, "I'm confident enough now. I'll go next" in the class. One after another, the other presenters did their thing at the front of the room and, finally, she had no choice. It was her turn, whether she liked it or not, whether she was confident or not.

The class I was teaching was three days long, and day three was presentation day. We'd spent *hours* learning those skills and tactics. Janet had all the information she needed to be fully prepared to step in front of the room. Still not *feeling* confident, she took her place at the head of the long conference table and began. One word at a time, she got going. As she said her first sentence and the world didn't crumble, she was able to say her second sentence. Then her third, and pretty soon she was six slides into her presentation and rocking the room like we'd never expected given what she'd told us and herself. She lit up. She was smiling and enjoying the power she had.

I stopped her and asked "Janet, how you feelin'?"

With big, round eyes—like she was surprised at what she was about to say—she said, "Actually, great! I feel . . . confident!"

If we wait to be confident in order to take a risk, we never will. Instead, flip the script, and tell yourself that action will produce confidence and get the flywheel going. *Do* the hard thing, and that will produce confidence.

I use these public speaking examples because they are visceral, vulnerable, and deeply somatic experiences. You can feel it right there in your body. Public speaking is a real-time feedback moment where the stakes feel incredibly high—no matter if you're talking to a room of ten or ten thousand. Equally visceral and somatic is the rush of confidence that comes when you do it—when you prioritize action over confidence. Then, those very public moments become life-changing experiences and produce self-trust—that delicious confidence factory that is action.

Action gets us unstuck. It breaks the logjam.

Action lets you just close the loop and say, "Between the chicken and the egg? The chicken came first. Let's move on."

It lets you move the rock so you can get out from behind that hard place.

It takes you away from being at sixes and sevens.

It loosens the grip.

It pulls you out of the rut.

It gets you off the ice.

But acting requires you to take the bigger risk to escape the confidence trap. Expect that when you act, confidence will follow.

IF NOT CONFIDENCE, THEN WHAT? PREPARATION.

I've declared that you don't need confidence to take action. You need action to create confidence you can accumulate.

So if you think you need confidence to act, and I've told you to act without confidence, then what do you need to act? You need preparation.

"I'm nervous." (Read: *I'm not confident.*)

"You're nervous? Are you prepared?"

"Yes."

"You know what to do?"

"Yes."

"You have your plan?"

"Yes."

"Do you trust your plan?"

"Yes."

"Did you practice?"

"Yes."

"You have your backup plan?"

"Yes."

"Still nervous?"

"Yes."

"Is there anything else to do?"

"No."

"So, you're prepared. Does that mean you're ready?"

"Yes."

The feeling of not being confident doesn't mean you're not ready. It's just how you *feel* about the action. We have a saying in our house that's crept into my communications coaching practice and into this book: It's OK to be nervous—do it *while* you're nervous.

SEPARATE CONFIDENCE FROM READINESS

So how will you know you're ready? You'll know you're ready when you can say, "I'm prepared." Preparation readies you for action, and action produces confidence.

> **It's OK to be nervous— do it while *you're* nervous.**

We are going to walk through how to build a rock-solid ask plan so you are prepared. This is your invitation to shift your goal from *feeling confident* to *knowing you are prepared and trusting that that preparation is enough to take action, knowing that the promise of confidence on the other side of action will draw you forward.* This is your invitation to seek out preparation instead of confidence. And sure, confidence is a side effect of preparation, but it's not the goal.

The great thing about seeking preparation instead of confidence is that it focuses you on something that is more concrete, material, and external. You can look at your work and writing as the evidence of your ready state and let the feelings about what you are about to do be present without them highjacking the whole damn trip you're about to go on toward your dream for yourself.

Your dream is worthy of action. So how do you prepare? Follow these steps.

Step 1: Make the Commitment

This is where you fall in love with your goal. You commit. You decide the pain is worth it, and you won't be talked out of pursuing the goal. You know now that the stakes are high enough to take the associated risks. You have a soundtrack in your head, and you can visualize yourself moving in slow motion—battling, striving, thoughtfully but intensely conversing—as you charge forward toward your goal. Labeling the failures as lessons. Batting away the rendezvous with uncertainty as a bump in the road, a flat tire, a vending machine that just won't cough up that Nutter Butter. But no, you will not be deterred. There is a way forward, and you see this challenge as the next hurdle to straddle, not a blockade.

Mkay? You've committed. You're all dressed up and looking for a place to go. What's next on your path to preparedness?

Step 2: Make the Plan

This is where you put together your schematics. Roll out the blueprint and plan your siege. In any scenario where confidence is thin but stakes are high, you need a plan. When I started auctioneering, I already had a strong and skillful presence on stage, but it was still scary because this was a new kind of stage. While I was fully committed, I needed a plan for the first auction I led. First, I'm going to take the stage, then I'm going to take a drink of water like I don't have a care in the world (*gulp*—metaphoric and real), and then I'll turn to the audience. Then, I'm gonna say the seven words I've planned to say to kick us off.

You're not just gonna bust onto the scene (via your ask) all committed but without a clear plan of action. You're not gonna just wing it. No sir. The planning is the preparation. The planning is the action-enabling exercise that you need to actually do the thing.

You're committed and you've got a plan, but is that enough? Not quite.

Step 3: Work the Plan

This is where you *werk werk werk werk werk werk* that plan: the script, the movements, the questions that might come up, the ways you'll answer, the boundaries you'll set, the exits you'll make. This is where you play out the *ifs* . . and *thens* . . . so you don't become paralyzed when the moment takes certain turns.

This is where you lay out your schematic on the table under a dim aluminum light shade, in the middle of a warehouse surrounded by kitted out MINI Coopers. This is where you scratch your chin and squint at the plan. This is where your best friend can ask, while possibly wearing some steampunk leather goggles, a scarf, and one of those ornate leather strap-on leg pockets for her iPhone, "Are you prepared?"

"Yes," you say with a knowing grin.

"How do you know?" she asks while whipping out her CBD-infused lip balm to protect against the *Mad Max*-esque desert that is the challenge before you. She knows you are going beyond the Thunderdome and wants to make sure you're ready. She doesn't care how confident you are; she cares that you're prepared. And she wants the facts.

"Well, I'm committed. Nothing will stop me. Not fear, not sadness, not Bob in Accounting. And I've got a plan. It's simple and clear and bulletproof. It's tied to our OKRs,* and the logic is obvious."

"Have you worked the plan?" Your BFF won't let you off the hook.

"I have. Within an inch of its life. It's been pressure tested, and it'll hold."

"Well, sounds like you're prepared," she returns her lip balm to its original holster.

"How do you feel?"

"I'm nervous. And I'm ready."

Aaaaaannnd, CUT!

WORK THE PLAN IN A WAY THAT WORKS FOR YOU

Every athlete has their routine to prepare for their big event—the breakfast they eat, the schedule they use to hydrate, the stretching and warm up exercises. These are the ways they work their plan. Every musician practices in a way that is unique to them, because that's the way they work their plan to make sure they're prepared for the moment when the lights go up.

---

* Objectives and Key Results (OKRs) are a common framework for corporate goal-setting.

I had my own way to work the plan I had for my time on stage at an auction. It included all kinds of weird things. Picking out my clothes the day before. Always exercising in the morning the day of the event. Writing out my script in longform, reading it aloud in my home's courtyard or at my office, pacing back and forth, filling up the space I have to work with to see how the script inspires—or doesn't inspire—a riff here and there, and where it calls for movement versus standing still, strong, and tall. Then comes the underlining of the key words that signal the idea I need to communicate in a script. Then, throwing the narrative parts of the script away because I'm prepared. Choosing and speaking, aloud, the first words that will come out of my mouth because I know that if I start strong, I'm OK. If I know what to do in the first ten seconds, I'll know what to do the rest of the time on stage. Still nervous, not perfectly confident, but ready because I've worked the plan in a way that works for me.

Here are some things you can do to work your plan and surround that plan with all the right scaffolding so you are ready *and* have belief in your readiness so you can act. There are two components to working your plan: scaffolding and practice. Let's start with scaffolding.

Scaffolding is what you might need around the ask you're about to make. The items listed below are things you can do to create the scaffolding that helps you work your plan and be prepared. These are ideas you can use as is, or you can customize them to fit you and your situation.

Your Threads

Pick an outfit that's right for you and the moment—the clothes you choose for the face-to-face ask or the email you need to draft must support the task at hand. It can be hard to write an *I'm a bad bitch*, ZOFO-ish email when you haven't showered and are still wearing your pajamas. Or maybe that's your jam! That whole *yeah, I'm in my slippers and sipping an Orange Crush don't-care* attitude is exactly what helps you send a fire email to the most ZOFO-ish people about ZOFO things. So put yourself in a set of threads that help you feel powerful, approachable, authoritative, eccentric, or whatever you need to feel to be ready to do the dance.

Your Soundscape

Music can elicit the vibes that help you prepare. It can reconnect you with yourself and with the moment you are about to step into. Make a playlist of the songs that put you in the state you want to be in when you walk into the big moment or the little moment that means a lot. Opera, metal, Femmetón, or your favorite Muppets classics—you know best which music supports the moment. Listen to it on your way to the gig to help you get prepared.

Your Persona

There is power in a persona. There are hundreds of personas available for you to draw on. The invitation to channel your inner [fill in the blank] is what I'm talking about here. But the persona you draw on doesn't need to be that of a big, well-known person—it can be one that's close to you or even a fictional character. Choose one that is useful for you, and channel that persona. When I'm preparing for an auction, knowing the persona I'm going to step into for my first words is key to being prepared. Sometimes I conjure the persona of a 1950s variety show host with glamour and wit, and sometimes I draw on the persona of a buttoned-up journalist who's all about business. Pick a persona that is most useful to you in that ask moment.

—

Great. That's scaffolding. Now let's talk about practice. This is when you workshop the content of the ask you are about to make and your plans of what to do when the ask turns into a negotiation. And you do it out loud. Learning takes place in your body, and if you need to be in a conversation to make the ask, you need to practice the conversation as part of your preparation. You can't just stare at your script and think about it, fantasizing about all the quick comebacks you'll have and the table flipping you'll do. No—you need to practice in a way that reflects the situation that you will actually be in. I am not an athlete, but, gulp, I am a softball mom (it's a thing), and there's a phrase they use in women's fast-pitch: practice like you play. So, practice is key. Here's how to do it.

Phone a Friend

"Hey, can I run through something with you?"

It's just that easy. Spending just fifteen minutes with a friend, saying, out loud, what you're gonna say in your ask, will do wonders for your preparation. But you don't just want to tell them *about* it, you want to actually *do* it. This is a lot less *first I'm going to talk about this and then I'm going to talk about that* and a lot more *here's what I'm going to say*. And then say it, just like you're going to say it. And then notice how it went.

When you phone a friend, get clear about what you want back from them. Feedback? Just listening? Direct edits to your script? A peptalk? Decide what you want from your friend so they know what role they are playing in your preparation.

WARNING: Don't phone the friend who always gives advice even when you don't want it. Call the people who can say, "Yep, I get what you want me to do. I got you."

Practice with that Persona

In scaffolding, you may take on a persona that's useful to you for stepping into your ZOFO and making the ask that matters. But your audience also has a persona—detail-oriented, coach-y and mentor-y, hard-hitting, skeptical and analytically minded, grumpy. If you are preparing to pitch your ask to a certain persona, find someone in your network who is a proxy, and practice with them. This'll give you the edge you need to know you're prepared. When I have to make a big ask to a harder hitting business type, I ask a *hard*-hitting business type to practice with me. Practice how you play.

Find Your Phrases

In many of the asks we'll make, there are critical pieces that require you have your shit together so you can hold the line. Like your reserve, for example. Or, for me, my first words are always a set up for how the rest of my time on stage goes, whether it's for an auction I'm leading or a keynote I'm giving. One great way to prepare is to find your phrases—the ones that let you hold that line. If you know now that it'll be a challenge for you to hold on to your reserve, decide now what you'll say when that reserve is challenged. What's the phrase you use that works for you? Examples you could make for yourself might be:

- "I can't say yes to that."
- "Thank you, but that won't work for me."
- "That's not something I can do."

Or maybe it's, "Seriously? Are you out of your gourd? There's no way in high heaven I'd say yes to that, and you know it. I can't believe you'd even counter with that, who do you think I am—and what do you think I'm doing here?" Use this one only if you are absolutely sure you're willing to block the boomerang effect. And if you're not? Then that is what you say on the inside, and on the outside it's, "No." And then breathe.

Or maybe it's simply: "Let me think about it," so you can buy yourself some time, take the pressure off yourself in the moment, and give yourself space to reply without feeling rushed. You can say this even if you know you're gonna say, "No, thank you," in the end.

Decide now the key phrases you'll use for those critical moments, and practice saying them.

—

So now you have three scaffolding things you can do to prepare for and support your ask and three ideas for practicing your ask. Craft your own versions of these steps and make them work for you. Notice what you've done before that worked for you—even if you sort of did it on accident. Now you can name and claim those scaffolding and practicing routines and make them part of your toolkit.

> **"**
> *Preparation unlocks action.*
> *Action unlocks confidence.*
> *Confidence accumulates.*
> **"**

Preparation unlocks action. Action unlocks confidence. Confidence accumulates. In our next chapter, you'll see that your plans don't always go as planned. And that's OK. What matters right now is that we've separated confidence from preparation and focused on action as the way to get into the ZOFO.

You can manufacture confidence through action. You don't have to wait for it to rain down; make it rain.

IT'S JOURNAL TIME! (Not the journaling type? Then just reflect—while you're waiting at the post office, staring out the window, packing a lunch, or browsing the forty-seven different types of yogurt you can choose from at the grocery store.)

Think about one thing you've done that you were scared to do but were prepared for and so you did it and it was great and built your confidence. Answer the following questions about that experience:

- How did you prepare? Why did that preparation work for you?
- How can you replicate that preparation in your life when you ready yourself for a big ask?
- What is one scaffolding step you can take every time you prepare to ask big?
- What is one practice step you can take every time you prepare to ask big?

CHAPTER 16

Other Things Can Happen When You Ask

There are so many metaphors for asking.

Asking is an adventure.

Asking is a treasure hunt—one ask at a time reveals something new and takes you on a journey.

Asking is a game of Clue, where every ask you make gives you information about where to go next and win the metaphorical board game of getting to your goals.

Asking is an archaeological dig where you excavate your potential and discover what's possible using asking as your hand trowel.

Along the way, like in each of these metaphors, surprising things can happen. You end up on adventures you didn't expect to take. You're surprised by the truths of what you find. You dig for fossils and instead uncover an ancient city. Sometimes it doesn't go the way you antici- pate or would have hoped for, and that's OK because the act of asking

> " *Every ask you make gives you information about where to go next.* "

produced and showed you something new that deepened your learning, clarified a strategy, rerouted you to a better path, or otherwise propelled you forward. Remember Jade the Champion from chapter twelve? This is exactly what happened to her.

Jade stepped into the idea of being an agent for her purpose to make a big ask. As the founder of a nonprofit designed to make world-class executive coaching available to women who are leaders in social impact, she had the opportunity to pitch, to a large company, a sponsorship program that would help create more financial sustainability for her nonprofit and its efforts. After she shared her pitch with me and we settled on the sponsorship rate (the dollars she'd be asking for), she committed to making the ask, and she made it.

Weeks later, I called to see how the pitch went. I was desperate to know if she got what she asked for, got a no and negotiated down, or if something else had happened.

Something else happened.

I called her up and here's how it went.

"Jade, I'm dying to know, how'd it go? What did'ya ask for?"

"I asked for $36,000, Dia," she said, sort of lightly.

"Whoa! That's even more than we discussed!" I was shocked. Not because it was such a big number, but because it was so much bigger than we'd planned.

"And?" I asked eagerly.

"They said no." She said, again, kinda lightly.

Now I was confused. I mean, I know I'm supposed to be the expert here, but I was confused by her reluctance to cough up the story and by how light she sounded about it all when I knew she took her nonprofit, shall we say, *not lightly*.

"Yep. They said no. And also to every increment and even to my reserve. They just said no to it all. And I feel really good about it. Know why, Dia? Because it really helped us figure out what we were missing."

During the conversation with the company she was pitching for the sponsorship, she mustered the courage to make the ask by being an agent for her purpose. The ask was a big one. But, turns out, it didn't matter how big it was.

Or how small! Why? Because the ask she made forced the company she was asking to realize they couldn't say yes to that number—or any other number. Because, organizationally, they had no social impact giving strategy. Without that, they wouldn't be able to rally their stakeholders and make a commitment.

Jade realized she and her team needed to do a better job vetting possible partnership and sponsorship candidates and get the right people and right companies into the conversation. Jade's ask made her and her team smarter. They'd been running on an assumption that everyone who took a meeting with them already had a giving strategy in place. Nope.

Jade went on, "So now? We are so smart about who we approach. We are vetting and curating our sponsors so we've got the right people in the room. We realized we were just barking up the wrong tree. Such a waste of time. But if we hadn't learned that lesson, we'd be spinning our wheels with all the wrong people."

> " *Even when things go wrong, other things can happen to make something else go right.* "

She asked, and something else happened that made her and her team smarter and more strategic going forward. That's not a loss; that's a huge gain. Even when things go wrong, other things can happen to make something else go right.

NEW IDEAS, NEW OFFERS, AND SURPRISING COLLABORATIONS

If you believe that the asks you'll make are the *beginning* of a conversation and that what you need is preparation, not unwavering confidence, to make substantial, big, and forward-moving asks, you may start to use asking as a success strategy, not just a special action reserved for the expected and ordained negotiation moments in your career, business, and life. Instead, when we are willing to take the risk of asking, we can discover what asking can yield beyond what we specifically request.

Jade made an ask that, in one perspective, yielded nothing. Zero dollars. She walked away with nothing—except she didn't. She walked away with new ideas. She experienced a constraint that showed her something new, an insight that illuminated something she was missing.

But new data and new ideas don't just come from getting a no. Our audiences and mentors and clients and all the other folks we extend our asks to are smart. And they have information we don't. When you expose them to your goals, they've got ideas about how you can reach them. Think back to the times you've made a request and the answer was, "Yes, I can do that—and while we're at it, have you thought about showing this to Frankie?"

As I sit here writing this for you, I can think of two moments in the last month where asks I've made produced new ideas about what I could do to advance the goal that was my reason for asking in the first place. And those ideas didn't come from me. They came from the person I was asking. And they did, nearly word-for-word, come into the conversation as "I can do that, and have you thought about [fill in kick-ass idea or person that will *totally* help get me where I'm going] . . .?"

In this way, asking is a way to harvest the best ideas from your professional community, both from established and new relationships.

And people *love* to share their ideas. Just flip the camera for a second. Imagine you're the one being asked. And in the set up for the ask, you understand really clearly what the person making the ask is trying to do and why *that* ask will help them do it. And in their set up, you see something super-duper obvious that you're not sure they've considered—a way of looking at the problem they're trying to solve, a connection or organization they should know about, another investor who'd be so into what they're doing, and so on. You offer those ideas, and BOOM! You've unlocked something new. You're an instant hero.

And adults love to have ideas. And they (ahem, we) love to share them. I mean, look around. How many of the folks in your professional or personal community won't shut up about their ideas? They've got ideas for everything, for fuck's sake! And mostly they're ideas for how other people should do something. So take advantage of that shit! Engage the smartest people you know with the asks you need to make, and watch the ideas roll in. I'm pretty sure at least one of the 37,655 ideas they share will lead to a massive breakthrough, helping you make connections and gain access to resources that can get you further down your path.

When we recognize that the people around us, especially professional and high-achieving people, love, love, love to share their smarts, we can begin tapping into a wellspring of opportunity we can't create on our own. You have the power to free those ideas using your ask as the trigger.

But it doesn't stop there. Another unexpected outcome of making a big, bold, strategic ask with enthusiasm, great storytelling (more on that later in the book), and courage, are the new offers you'll receive. Sometimes our audiences love to share ideas, and sometimes those ideas turn into offers you didn't even know were a possibility.

I sat in on a call recently talking about a project. The woman on the other side of the call was someone I reached out to because I had a very specific ask. In our chatting and getting-to-know-you part of the conversation, we built enough rapport to get down to business. I set up the vision of what I was trying to do and then laid out my ask. She was a quick yes (that was fine cuz this wasn't a ZOFO-type of moment for me) and then asked me, "Have you considered [fill in idea]?"

And I was like, "Actually, thank you for bringing it up. Yes, I have considered that idea but not for a long time. It's interesting you bring it up as it's probably time I put that back on the table." I was kinda stunned because she was reviving a thought I'd had before, which was super validating, and through her sharing her idea, all of a sudden my understanding of what she looks for, how she makes connections, and what playing field she's on shifted. Like, in a good way. Who I was dealing with started to be so clear to me. All. Good. News. For both of us.

Quickly she added to her idea: "I bring this up because I think it would be really powerful for you, and we produce the event where that would happen. Would you be interested in participating?"

HELLZ YEAH I AM! I mean, all chill and shit, I said, "Thank you so much for the invitation. Let me get with my team, and if you send the details, we'll respond by the end of the week."

My ask triggered a new idea and that triggered an offer I hadn't anticipated. This is my tiny story, but I'm sure this has happened to and for you before. And it likely will again. Name it. Claim it. And notice, again, that asks can do a lot of heavy lifting for you, if you want to use them. Sometimes, if you want to double down on the archaeological metaphor I started with, they work like a small shovel than uncovers the corner of something new—and other times, asks are like a big-ass excavator that shows you a world lost in time.

THE SOURCE OF ALL THE EXTRA

In this chapter we're talking about how things we didn't anticipate can happen when we ask—the bonus pack you didn't even know you wanted. So do these extras just happen? Do I just say, "Hey, can I have that gumball?" and then the sky opens up and ideas and offers and surprising collaborations rain down?

Nope. The best ideas, offers, and collaborations that come from an ask are sourced from the kind of storytelling that paints a clear picture of where you are going and that helps your audience see what you see. It comes from the type of signaling you do that sends a message of who you are, what your goals are, and what matters to you; and from the clarity you have about what you want and how you envision the path to getting it. Asking is not demanding. It's not firing off an ask like a cannonball through a wall. We're not stepping onto the scene, screaming to speak to the manager. You're not on a SWAT team.

No, you are bringing someone into your world and inviting them to share in your reality as context for the ask you are about to make. You are storytelling, creating a clear vision for someone else to engage with so they can see how your ask fits into something greater.

And it's in that set up, in that painting of a picture, that ideas can start firing, leading to an "Oh, I see what you're trying to do. This gives me an idea!"

That vision you are creating, and every detail in it, stimulates thinking and connections and possibility. So choose the details carefully—the names you invoke, the descriptors you use, the parts of the story you highlight, the emphasis you place on the picture you're painting. The setup is the spark that ignites possibility.

A few years ago I was giving a workshop for Project: Ask Like an Auctioneer. I was talking with the organizer of the event, and we were discussing whether someone needed to always get what they asked for. And we both agreed the answer was no, not always. And that fact didn't cancel out the importance of making an ask that is in our ZOFO. To challenge, and actively go for what you know they'll say no to. Excited, she told me a story of a woman who'd done just that.

"Someone in my network just did this very thing we're talking about, Dia. She's a Black woman who went for a CEO role at a mid-sized, VC-backed firm. It was a big job and her first time in this role. She asked big, Dia. In her comp package, for a number that flips the script. She got a no. The board just wasn't going to go for it. But they heard her, and it triggered a discussion. She'd signaled to them where her sights were set. And because her comp and performance are related, her key stakeholders knew that if she was in a position to make that kind of coin, she'd be performing at a level they wanted to see happen. She signaled where she saw herself, and that was generative."

So they had ideas on what she could do to be in the place where that kind of package could be a reality. They made offers on how they could support her in getting there and collaborated with her to design a pathway and a plan that brought the organization to the level that would have them say yes to that kind of compensation package at a future date. She did the signaling needed to let her audience see where she saw herself. And all the ideas, offers, and collaboration from there embraced what she signaled were to be set as the parameters for the conversation.

The exercise of crafting an ask that is right for your goals is an act of self-reflection and clarification. When we ask ourselves what our goals are, and then challenge ourselves to craft the asks that get us there, we may, as we try to line those up, have to take a second look at our goals and have an honest conversation about what we want. When we get clear on that, the storytelling for that ask and the ask itself is so aligned that the ideas, offers, and collaborations we receive as a result of that are also aligned with what we truly want. Clarity creates alignment. Alignment creates more generative and high-quality ideas, offers, and collaborations.

Supriya the Thoughtful joined one of our post-workshop coaching circles. A lead at a global company, she came to the circle thinking she wanted a new title that came with a promotion and people management. After digging into the why behind her goal, she looked a layer deeper into her life and dreams for herself and realized, no, she didn't much care about the title and promotion. What she was really looking for was more collaboration on elite projects that let her work in innovation. She'd assumed that would come with a promotion and a specific title, and that people management was just going to come with the package. She said she wanted to manage a team because managing a team came with the job she thought she needed to get to do more of the innovation work she craved. In her reflection she reframed her goal from *be a manager* to *be an individual contributor working on innovation*, which, in turn, changed her ask.

Clarity of goal means alignment in the ask, who you ask, the story you tell about the ask, and the signals you send around the ask.

When Supriya the Thoughtful saw for herself what she really wanted and not what she thought she needed to want, a relaxed and relieved look came over her face. We could all see in the call that she had woken up to something for herself that gave her clarity. And that clarity is contagious. When we are clear on what we're asking for and why, we spark something in others that can be the source of ideas, offers, and surprising collaborations that make the journey of asking the ride of your life and a surprising adventure.

Gabby's story is her mom's story—and is our story too. Gabby was a young artist. Lorella, Gabby's mom, slid into my DMs and shared the story below. A few years later, what she shared with me has slid into this book. This text exchange, edited for clarity and privacy, is an example of two ideas in this book. One: that when we ask for more and get it, we can change everything for everyone. Two: other things can happen when we ask.

Lorella:

Story time.

Gabby has a passion for drawing and animating. COVID has made life pretty lonely, but she found an app that's a community of artists that support each other. They ask each other to draw things in exchange for coins.

She came to me and asked for advice one day. I was new to the app and figured it was like a video game chat room. But it was a real marketplace.

Anyway, she was frustrated and tells me someone requested her art but was offering well below what she sells it for. My ears obviously perked up as I have been highly trained and influenced by you in such matters. 😂

Her baseline was 250 coins. The offer that was made was 117 coins (the buyer was transparent about how much they had on hand). She was frustrated because she said it's a lot of work to do what they want and her price is already a bargain. I asked her what she wanted to do? She said, "I want them to pay me what I am asking for."

I said, "OK, let them know nicely that your art has been priced, and they can come back when they have what you're asking for."

Dia:
OMG

Lorella:

Then I thought about it and said, *Well . . . why don't I show her how to negotiate a little?* I said, "Would you like to draw them something else for fewer coins? Maybe something that isn't as time-consuming? You could still earn one hundred coins."

Dia:

Right? "I don't go on sale, but I can reduce scope."

Lorella:

She said, "Like what?"

I said, "Maybe an emoji or an avatar?"

And she said, "Oh, I can make a sticker pack. It doesn't take up a lot of time."

"Great! Are you happy with that?" I asked. "Maybe this will open the door for when they do have 250 coins. They will remember you."

She went off and negotiated. Turns out the sticker pack wasn't going to work—something about how the tech works—so the project was a no-go.

The teenager knew her reserve, committed to her baseline, passed on a lowball offer (her words, not mine), and then, later on that day, got featured on the app and gained 150 more followers (celebrity status for teens). She was much happier.

Dia:
Fucking a.
Lessons.
OK, this is literally choking me up.

Lorella:
So if a young woman in her teens on an app can do this, grown ass women and men can do it. But I truly wonder if it's us influencing her or was she born this way or were we all born this way but somehow lose this while we grow up?

Dia:
It's taught.
This is a skill. A mental framework.
She was frustrated, and then you gave her a framework to take her power back.

Lorella:
But I've held this story for about a month, and I keep forgetting to pass it along.
It was dark and late and I might have cried a little myself. This stuff has the power to change so many people and multiple generations.

Dia:
Crying.
This is what I mean by "change everything for all of us." If you are making it possible for your daughter to hold on to what she values—boom! Intergenerational impact!

Lorella:
There's a list of stuff I want for Gabby—and that moment checked off one of those items.

Gabby asked like an auctioneer and something else happened. Lorella changed everything.

IT'S JOURNAL TIME! (Not the journaling type? Then just reflect while you're gardening or walking the dog or scrubbing the tub or puttering to the corner store for an Almond Joy.) Answer the following questions:

- What is something in your life or work you thought would go one way, but it went another direction, and yet it was all OK?
- What did you learn?
- When did you learn it?
- What did you do differently after?

CHAPTER 17

The Four Categories
of Strategic Asks

I nitially, I thought this whole asking like an auctioneer thing would only apply to asks centered on money. But nope.

In chapter one, I promised I'd share the four types of strategic asks we can make. Remember when Moira the Muse said, "If you don't recognize all the asks we have to make on our path to fulfilling our professional potential, you're missing it"? She was right, and over the course of the next few years and few hundred conversations around how to ask for more and get it, I learned that every ask we make can fall into one (or more) of four categories:

- Money
- Influence
- Authority
- Balance

I'll get into each in a sec. But first, a little story about mountain biking.

I'm in the business of connecting ideas. I mean, look at this book you're reading right now—who would think we could take auctioneering and apply its strategies to your serious-as-a-heart-attack goals? And the way I make connections like these is by letting what a former colleague calls "the guys in the back room" do some work. These guys are the little thinking elves that get to work when you're resting and not doing stuff that uses your brain in a hard-core, problem-solving way. You know, that thinking time that happens when you're waiting in the Group B line with seventy-nine other passengers, all praying to get overhead storage when you load onto the plane. This thinking happens when you're walking the dog or cooking or going for a long run, or whatever else you do that lets your mind wander.

For me, it's engaging in things that are physically demanding, but lower in required skill—running up the side of a mountain or lifting heavy things and then putting them down and picking them up again over and over. Or, engaging in things that require absolutely zero physical demand and zero skill. Things like sitting in a chair, lying in bed and staring out the window, sitting on the stoop and watching cars go by. Think about the activities you do that allow your mind to wander, because I'll be asking you to make some connections soon for yourself. I want to invite you to notice how you get insights—what contexts or activities let *your* guys in the back room do some connecting work for you.

It was a beautiful day, and I was out with my husband on a mountain bike ride. The sky was blue, the air felt warm on my skin, and we were pushing our way along a soft, pine needle–cushioned trail along a lake in a forest in Northern California. The guys in the back room woke up and started to confer with one another. My thinking elves were having a board meeting.

In the last two years, I'd spoken with hundreds of women who were trying to make moves. Moves that would advance them toward their goals. And often, settling into our workshop and keynotes, they assumed we'd be talking about salary negotiation and things limited to whatever was money-adjacent. Nope. Moira the Muse was right.

In workshops and keynote Q&As, together my audiences and I devised ask plans for women running for office for the first time, women who saw that, while asking a respected and well-connected business leader in the community for a campaign donation was a good move, a better one was asking for that leader to host a campaign event or loan-gathering space and/or endorse and connect the candidate to new voters.

I had spoken to women who were changing their lives whole hog and were seeing that the path to that change was via asking for a new type of work that pointed them in the right direction.

Women had designed asks that would help them get into rooms where decisions were being made, get in front of the right audiences, gain the sponsorship of another influential voice in their industry, receive shares instead of cash, add *one* simple word to a job title that would create the platform for their next decade of financial and career growth, remove tasks and responsibilities from a project or role such that the work they were saying yes to could be a platform for success by being just the right size and including just the right things based on their goals.

We can ask for more than what's on the menu. And when we do, we're asking strategically.

The guys in the back room that were percolating on this bike ride could see women were asking for so much more than money alone. And they started wrestling with the question, *If we had to organize these ask-types, you know, to make it easier to see, what would the categories be?*

They looked for patterns. Surveyed the land. And BOOM! They sent me the message:

Four. There are four. Every strategic ask we've helped women craft could fall into one or more of the following:

> " *We can ask for more than what's on the menu. And when we do, we're asking strategically.* "

1. **Money.** Money asks involve all the things related to making the big bucks: salary, freelancing rates, project proposal prices, stock options, cuts of the profit, commissions, affiliate payment terms, donations, loans, venture capital, angel funding, and so on.

2. **Influence**. These are the asks that we make that grow our influence in our market, network, organization, peer group, or professional community. Think: asking to speak on behalf of your project team at your company's all-hands meetings, asking to be the MC of a panel in your industry, speaking on influential stages, securing mentorship, asking for sponsorship, gaining access to networks, getting an introduction to that *one* person who can help with that *one* thing you need to reach a goal, getting publicity in the right channel, building partnerships, and the list goes on.

3. **Authority.** These are the asks that add to your power to *author* your life, increasing your ownership of decision-making. Think: to get promoted to a role that gives you authority to choose what happens on your team or in this or that project, to be added as a stakeholder in a critical project, to change the way you work so you are the architect of your day's schedule, to add your name as a byline or in the credits (this one also touches influence), and the list goes on. If it feels or sounds or looks like something that would give you more authority, you can ask for it.

4. **Balance.** This one isn't about work-life balance. It has more to do with bringing into balance your outer context and your inner self so you can live a life that is reflective of who you actually are. Women I've worked with have made asks that make it possible to: work with more autonomy, take a sabbatical so they can live abroad for a season or a year, move from employee to contractor status so they can have more freedom, change careers all together, move from one function to another in their company so they can do work that reflects their actual interests, and more. All these kinds of asks bring into balance who we are, the work we do, and the life we live.

When those guys in the back room shot me this message, I pulled over fast. As the executive in the room, I concurred with the team and quickly wrote these down so that, later—now—you can use them as a way to think about the asks you *could* make if you are going to use asking as a success strategy and if you are going to ask like an auctioneer.

In the next chapter, you'll learn a six-step process for building powerful strategic asks. It's a fun and easy process. And if you're ever stuck, you can ask yourself: *If I needed to ask for something to help me reach my goal, would I ask for more money, influence, authority, or balance?*

To help you use these four types of asks to achieve your goals, do the following exercise:

> Look back on your career and business, and identify an ask you've made that was critical. Something you asked for in your past that made a difference to a goal you had. If you had to put this ask into one category, where would it fit?

Remember the simple ask I made years ago that changed everything: "Will you teach me?"

Looking back now, I see that this ask was one that gave me more authority in my career path and brought more balance. I was going to learn tools and skills that gave me more choices and made me feel like I was authoring my own life. And it was an ask that wholeheartedly brought my outside life into balance with my inside self.

In the next chapter, as we build out a strategic ask for you, don't thank me; thank the guys in the back room.

IT'S JOURNAL TIME! (Not the journaling type? Then just reflect while you're darning your socks, hanging out your laundry, polishing the family silver, or sweeping the stoop in preparation for your besties who are coming for dinner.)

Think about which of the four categories of asking—money, influence, authority, or balance—get you most excited. Consider:

- What's exciting about it/them?
- What will you be able to do if you have more of the category you want?
- How would those resources help you reach your current goal(s)?

CHAPTER 18

Your Most Powerful Ask

A t this point, you've got a firm grasp on how to ask like an auctioneer. You've got nine ideas and strategies to help you find the courage to ask for more, advance your ask when it's stuck, and step into your own personal ZOFO. And we've addressed some of the blockades, alternative outcomes, and key questions people like you often have. Here's a quick recap of the ideas behind and strategies for making your most powerful asks:

1. **Idea:** People are irrational, or *their* rationale is not *your* rationale.
   Strategy: Don't decide for your audience what they'll say "yes" and "no" to. Let them decide.
2. **Idea:** Know your reserve.
   Strategy: Always identify the minimum you'll accept so *you* know exactly what *you'll* say "yes" and "no" to.
3. **Idea:** Increments matter.
   Strategy: Don't just split the difference on the dollars. Plan your increments, and know what increments you have to plan.
4. **Idea:** Are you in, or are you out?
   Strategy: Make people decide so you know where you stand and can move on.

5. **Idea:** Price is a measure of value, not of absolute worth.

   Strategy: Read the response you get from an ask as a measure of how the person you are asking values something, not as a measure of its absolute worth. Do this as a way to depersonalize the asks you make and the *noes* you get.

6. **Idea:** Your market is bigger than the room.

   Strategy: Keep an abundance mindset to allow you to risk getting a no, knowing that there are other markets for your ask.

7. **Idea:** Purpose is a source of courage.

   Strategy: Get clear on your purpose, and use that to fuel your courageous asks.

8. **Idea:** Be an agent for your purpose.

   Strategy: Act on behalf of your purpose in order to advocate for it with more freedom and less fear.

9. **Idea:** Inside every ask is an offer.

   Strategy: Find that offer to sell your ask for the highest bid.

Maybe right now is a good time to circle whichever one or more of these strategies resonates most with you. The ones that scream "Me, me, me! Up here in the nosebleeds!" Give that idea some love and highlight it. It may be the one you lean on going forward.

YOU'VE GOT FUEL: IT'S TIME FOR AN ASK PLAN

You don't have a specific ask in mind? Don't worry. In this chapter, we're going to move through a simple process to design a powerful ask whether you have one in mind or not. I know you're sitting here, reading all these words and feeling kind of excited and thinking, *I can't wait for my next negotiation.* I want to give you the opportunity to ask like an auctioneer without having to wait. Because this stuff *is* exciting! One woman once said to me, "I've never been so excited to set myself up for rejection!"

Yeah, I get it. I live it too. Now that I'm asking like an auctioneer (even when I'm not auctioneering), it's kinda sticky—it sticks in my mind and I almost actively look for reasons to ask like an auctioneer. It becomes, dare I say, fun! Like hitting a golf ball off a tee just right (I hate golf, but I'll crush a ball off a tee at a driving range once in a while) or like cracking the hard shell of a crème brûlée or like eating potato chips. You start, and ya just can't stop. There's something super compelling about activating your auctioneer self and experimenting to see what you can get. There's a real adrenaline rush and dopamine surge that comes with the surprise and adventure of seeing what asking for more does. There's power in

> **"*I've never been so excited to set myself up for rejection!*"**

the *Hmm, that didn't work. Here's what I'm going to do now.* There's richness in activating your confidence with action instead of waiting for it to come to you—a recognition that our desire for confidence need not hold us hostage, but instead that acting can propel us forward to uncover what we need to get to our goals *and* help us build confidence along the way. There is joy in a great asking experiment. And yes, there is disappointment. There is sadness. There are those days when the speed bump of a hard no or a ghosting feels like a mountain of shale rock that's sliding down with every step you take toward the peak. Those days when you'll have to remember that your market is bigger than the room and it's time to move to a new conversation, a new audience, a new possibility.

And there is loss. There are moments when you will see that if you can't get your reserve met, it's time to make a change—the kind of change that carries such loss: change of job, change of team, change of plans, just *change*. But in that, you can know that when you make the bold choice to ask like an auctioneer, when you make the bold choice to act on what you've decided you'll do when your reserve isn't met, you're standing up for yourself, for your dream, and for what matters and is possible for you—in your relationship with the world, but on your terms.

But you'll get there. Asking like an auctioneer means adopting asking as a success strategy. And trusting that while there is no guarantee you'll ask for more and get it *this* time, you will ask for more and get it *over* time.

THERE'S NO NEED TO WAIT

One of my communications coaching clients has an awesome operating principle we call "The Shin Guard Principle."

> *Asking like an auctioneer means adopting asking as a success strategy.*

Today, as I'm writing this book, she is a founding CEO of a VC-backed company, but when she was a kid—like seven or so—she was a soccer player.

One day, she and her father were driving somewhere through their town, nestled low in the mountains, and got stuck in the snow. Her dad freaked out. Huffing and chuffing, he kicked the tires and considered the options (this was pre-cell phone era, FYI). I'm sure he's a nice guy—he was just pissed.

Meanwhile, my client, in her full seven-year-old entrepreneurial mode, rifled through the trunk of the car and pulled out a shin guard.

"What are you doing? Stop wasting time! We're stuck—we have to figure out how to get a truck out here to pull us out."

She ignored her dad and started digging. One shin guard scoop at a time, she cleared the snow and packed it down and begged her dad to try—just once—to get the car out.

In one rev of the engine, they were dislodged.

And that's the Shin Guard Principle: find tools and use them in ways they weren't intended to be used.

She didn't wait for a tow truck. Didn't wait for a pick up. She invented a way to unstick what was stuck.

You don't have to wait either. You don't have to wait for that next known negotiation to ask like an auctioneer. You can invent asks that will help you reach your goals. You can use asking as a success strategy.

YOUR MOST POWERFUL ASK PLAN IN SIX STEPS

In this chapter we're going to learn to build a rock-solid ask plan in six simple steps using the Your Most Powerful Ask Plan framework. This will give you a way to apply everything we've learned so far.

In my workshops, I've helped hundreds of women build a strategic ask and then ask it like an auctioneer. Everyone from tech leaders looking to deploy new site reliability technologies across high-profile projects to women starting nonprofits to women looking to elevate their income or take that road trip they've always dreamed of. Women have used their iterations of the Most Powerful Ask Plan to identify and craft asks that get them better titles, mentorship, access to networks, and introductions that can change everything.

And you can make your own powerful ask too. Let's go.

Step 1: The Goal

We don't start with an ask. Because your ask is really about gaining something you need to get to where you want to go, you need to know where you're heading. So your first step is identifying a clear, mid-term goal. One that's easy to see when you've attained it. We don't want vague goals like *keep learning* or *grow as a leader*. We need concrete goals that are measurable. Some examples of concrete, measurable goals are:

- Form a board of directors with five industry experts who can advance the business through their network.
- Elevate my income by 30 percent in the next eighteen months.
- Get the word "manager" in my title in the next twelve months.

- Work in the innovation lab on a project with visibility across four specific teams.

In the previous chapter, we noted the four goal categories you can choose from. (Quick reminder: the categories are money, influence, authority, and balance.) Notice if the goal you're building an ask plan around falls into one of those categories. If not, great. If so, also great. If you're stuck a bit on naming a goal, ask yourself if a goal in one of the four goal categories might seem right for you.

Now, before we move to the next step, let's take a beat right here because goal-shame is real. Before we build out your ask plan, take a look at your goal and notice if you feel like it's the wrong one. Not because it's the wrong one for you, but because it's not big enough, fancy enough, or it's not part of your expected career trajectory. Notice if you're already looking at it and going, *I shouldn't have that goal. I should have one that looks like this or looks like that.*

Stop. You get to want what you want. There's no goal-shaming here. This is a goal-shame-free zone. If you're struggling to embrace the goal you have, it might help to know that, while we have four goal *categories*, there are also three goal *types* we can name and claim. They are recognition goals, experiential goals, and mastery goals.

Recognition goals are goals tied to something that includes a symbol of recognition. A medal, trophy, title, or maybe making a "best of" list. It's that goal type that evokes that feeling of publicly winning. It's something recognizable in the world and works like a badge. Maybe your goal is to win a pitch competition in the next eighteen months. Or to be named the top sales leader in your company this year. Maybe it's time for a promotion to a title that gives you a level up that can't be overlooked. If you're looking at your goal, or if you're looking for a goal to choose, and this goal seems right? Great! And if there's a whisper of *I shouldn't be so ambitious*, silence that voice because you get to want what you want.

Experiential goals are closely tied to the kinds of experiences you want to have. One year, I was having a drink with a client. She's a senior executive who could go higher in her organization if she wanted to. But she doesn't.

She said to me, "I don't really have a goal. I just want to live quietly and spend time with my family, go on vacation, and not take on too much." She said this as if somehow her goal of "live quietly and spend time with my family, go on vacation, and not take on too much" isn't a real goal. As she said it to me, her voice was low and she looked crestfallen. I could smell goal-shame in the air. She'd shamed it so hard, she'd made it not real.

"Um, that sounds like an experiential goal to me. You just said that that kind of life is what you want. Is that not a goal?"

The moment she heard that term—*experiential goal*—I could see her face light up. We spent the next few minutes talking about how to shape that picture into a more concrete goal. Does it mean "I don't work on Fridays," or does it have other concrete components she could name? And how she could shape a named goal informed by her goal type? In the next twelve to eighteen months, could she reduce the scope of her role by 20 percent, for example? Now that's a goal! As we talked about her goal of living a quiet life, we looked at how balanced or unbalanced her external context was with her internal desire. And then she pinpointed what needed to happen and what to ask for to move those more into harmony. See how it's all coming together here?

Mastery goals having nothing do with badge-able events or leveling up publicly. There are no promotions involved or accolades. These goals are not about lifestyle or experiences like bungee jumping or hiking the Pacific Crest Trail or living in a tree house. They're all to do with becoming great at something.

One woman shared her truth in a coaching circle I facilitated: "Truth is, I don't really want to go for a promotion. I don't care to manage people. It's the logical next step in my career. I guess I've had that on my goals list because my manager suggested it and I'm just kinda going along with it. Instead, what I really want, even in my mid-career, is to be an individual contributor and be the expert in my field here." Her goal type? Mastery. So we then crafted a goal around that type that elevated her visibility as an expert—and fell under the influence category.

So many of us blow off our pursuits of mastery as just extra hobbies, as if being good at something and wanting to be the best isn't enough. "To make it in the world, you need to promote! Build! Manage!" . . . But those goals aren't always ours. Mastery goals are about becoming the trusted source, the expert. They're about becoming so skilled at or knowledgeable about a thing that you can recognize your own mastery. It's about the joy that comes with depth over breadth. And, for some, this *is* the mountain to climb and the goal to set. We revere violinists who are masterful in their craft. But if we want to be masterful in agile project management, we can easily get pulled onto a path toward recognition goals when all we really want is to master something for the sake of mastering it.

You get to want what you want.

You can use goal types and categories to help navigate and articulate what you really want. It can be really useful to use types and categories to name and claim goals that you have, because without them your goals can just whiz right by you. So. Using the four goal categories and the three goal types, capture a mid-term, concrete goal about which you can say, "Yes. That's what I want."

Step 2: The Move

What's *one* big move you need to make to get you closer to your goal?

This step is critical to finding an ask that matters to you. It's easy to skip this step. Don't. The move is the thing that you need to act on in order to get closer to your goal. And there can be lots of different moves that get you closer to a goal that you care about. So what we want to do here is take inventory of all the different kinds of moves you could make that get you closer to that goal—and then pick one to design an ask around. You can imagine that at the top of a pyramid is your goal and that beneath that you could have 567 big moves that help you get there. And underneath each of those big moves, you could design an ask that helps activate the move that gets you closer to your goal.

So let's imagine that you want to have the word "manager" in your title within the next eighteen months. This would be an authority category goal and a recognition goal. Or it may be in the balance goal category as you want to bring into balance the work you do and who you are. Or an experiential goal for you as you're looking for a daily experience of supporting and encouraging people. You can frame it however you like.

So, maybe one next big move you could make is a move that would help you demonstrate specific competencies that set you up for a manager role. Let's think: What if you, in the next eighteen months, got to be in charge of a cross-functional project or a project that requires a cross-functional team *and* to lead and manage that project in a way that demonstrates the same competencies required of a manager of a team of direct reports? So that when it comes time for performance review, or comes time for an opportunity to ask for that promotion, you've already made a big move that allowed you to demonstrate why you are right for a manager role. Look at your goal and ask yourself: *What might be a big move I could make that would help advance me toward my goal?*

Charlotte wanted to be VP of marketing. She knew taking on more responsibility and demonstrating her competencies in areas necessary for, or at least adjacent to, the VP role she was aiming for would be critical if she was going to make it to that position one day.

Her next big move was to own an entire event strategy for the year for the organization she was working for. She didn't want to just be a key contributor, stakeholder, or strategist on the team, but to actually own the events strategy. And the events themselves included everything from budget to design to execution for the marketing function. She knew the events strategy was high profile and that if she successfully owned and executed a strategy that mattered to the business, she'd be well positioned for and much closer to achieving the goal that she had in mind for herself.

So, for her, the big move was to own that next calendar year's worth of event strategies.

My mission here is to help one million women ask for more and get it by using asking as a success strategy based on what I learned from my impact hobby of fundraising auctioneering. And I knew one goal was to, partnered with a publisher, write a book.

So I knew my next big move was to secure an agent who knew exactly where to send the book that you're reading right now. That was my very next big move I needed to make on my path to achieving the goal of publishing the book that you have in your hands or in your ears right now. My move, at that stage, was pretty obvious. Your next best move may be really obvious, or it could take a little imagination.

There are so many moves that could materially advance you toward your goals. Make a list of potential moves you could make right now. When you have that list, circle the one or the few that feel the most right, true, and exciting to you right now.

Now you've completed step two of your Most Powerful Ask Plan.

Step 3: The Ask

What is your ask?

Finally, you're prepared to design your ask. This is my favorite part because it's like we're getting ready to go shopping. Think of all the things we *could* get! We can wonder about what's possible, we can guess what we might find, we can browse our imagination and think of all the possibilities. In this step, we let ourselves dream a bit. You can start with "who" questions and wander through your mental Rolodex for people you know who might spark thoughts about what you might ask them. Or, you can flip it and start with a "what" question, rolling around in your mind all the things you could ask for, and then you can start connecting those things with who can help you get them. It might go something like: "Who do I know who's in this field, related function, network, or topic area, and what could I ask them for that might activate my big move that gets me closer to my goal?"

Or it might be like: "Hmm, what might I ask for that helps me activate that move, and who do I know that is perfect to help me do it?"

As you dream up the asks you could make, here are a few things to note to get your flywheel going:

Let there be many asks. Notice how we've done a little work to get us here. We've identified our goal. We've identified the move or a shortlist of moves. And as you identify your asks, you might find that, like your moves, there are three, four, or five asks you could make. There are always multiple asks you could make to help activate that move that gets you closer to your goal. We're brainstorming and finding the one that looks, sounds, and feels most right. You'll make a list and then pick the ask to make now.

Your ask can be about what you know or don't know. Your big ask might be to be involved with a very specific project that you know is in the pipeline. Maybe you're asking for executive sponsorship from three leaders in your organization to help uncover and identify what a potential project might be. Maybe you're asking to participate in strategy meetings that you usually don't get access to so that you yourself can surface what the next big project is that you feel would be perfectly aligned to the goal of becoming a manager of people.

Find the ask that activates the move that brings you closer to your goal.

And like the other two steps in this process, let yourself brainstorm a little bit.

I made so many ZOFO-style asks to make it possible for me to find the right publisher that brought this book project to life. Along the way, I knew there was a publisher out there, and the kinds of asks I made for months were about bringing this project to the right people, growing my network, gaining access to mentorship, and receiving advice from people who were out of my reach, all of whom supported me as I pursued this project from ideation to proposal and beyond.

And don't forget to include who you're asking as part of your ask plan. That can be either a person or a persona. It might be that there's a certain type or profile of person or organization that you need to make an ask of. It may be that you know exactly who would be the perfect person to ask for the thing that you need in order to move closer to your goal. So your ask plan includes planning for both *what* you might ask for and *who* you might ask it of.

Determine those two things, and then draft the ask in a clear way, like below:

- I could ask to be part of our regular roadmap meetings so I can discover upcoming strategic cross-functional projects and be first to volunteer to participate in them.
- I could ask to lead an upcoming project I already know is in the plan.
- I could ask my mentor to suggest me as a leader for upcoming projects.

Once you've got a nice list of the asks you could make, circle the one that resonates with you most. You've brainstormed a solid little list, and now you can cherry-pick the sweetest one.

Step 4: The ZOFO

Now it's time to get clear on how to make your ask as big as it can be. What is the ZOFO version of your ask? You've got a big goal and an opportunity to make a move that can help you make great strides in your journey toward that goal. Challenge yourself, and make sure the size of the ask places it right in your ZOFO. You don't want to leave an opportunity on the table. Maybe the ZOFO version means the cross-functional project team needs to: (1) include ten people, (2) have visibility across four key functional groups, and (3) qualify to be on the agenda of your company all-hands to give you visibility.

Feel bigger now? This is where we find the biggest version of the ask. And you'll know it's big if it: (1) threatens getting a no, (2) makes you feel like you're going to be in the ZOFO when you ask for it, and (3) is exciting.

So sit back and ask yourself: *What would make this ask a ZOFO one?*

You may find you're making a component of the ask bigger. Like, the ZOFO version of the ask is for 25 percent more than the shares I was already asking for. Or maybe it's an add-on. Like, maybe what makes your ask a ZOFO ask is adding on a communications component—that you are the communications lead on the project and the spokesperson so you get visibility too, which *really* gives your move a boost.

And don't freak out about thinking *too* big; we haven't asked for anything yet. Just saying this stuff out loud doesn't mean you've decided what you'll ask for. Nobody is listening to your brainstorming. Actually, if this ZOFO version of the ask feels a little transgressive, a little naughty, and a little exciting—you're in the ZOFO, so, welcome!

Step 5: The Reserve

You know your ZOFO ask—now it's time to get clear on the minimum you'll take. It's time to get clear on and set your reserve. What is the minimum counteroffer you'll take?

Notice I don't use the word "settle" here. We're not settling for anything. We're deciding now what we'll say yes to. It's a different vibe. *Settling* is like (insert eyeroll and slouched over dining room table floppy body), "OK, fiiiin-nne." *What I'm willing to say yes to* is a lot more like (insert sitting up straight with fancy pen in hand) "Yes. That works for me." *We're* setting our reserve.

Sometimes your reserve has a few components. For example, what's the smallest version of that cross-functional project team you want to lead that still makes it worth it to you and advances your big move? Maybe your re-serve: (1) includes a minimum of six people, (2) has visibility across two key functional groups, and (3) is on the agenda of your engineering all-hands to give you visibility. Smaller audience than company all-hands, but still great visibility.

Setting your reserve compels you to be honest with yourself. Look for that balance of minimum and happiness. We *do not*, I repeat, *do not* want to say "yes" to something we actually want to say "maybe" or "I guess so" to. Knowing your reserve helps you zero in on an amount to agree to in terms of a job, partnership, or collaboration. Because if you accept terms that you feel shitty about, you may end up in a deal you wish you weren't part of. And that helps no one.

So show up to the task of setting your reserve with honesty and integrity. Setting your reserve is a courageous act. I mean, think about it: when we ask, we're scared someone might say no. But tables are turned when you set a reserve—you're the one with the power. You get to say no to something too!

So what's the minimum counteroffer you'll say yes to? Ask yourself and make a list using the following prompt: "The minimum I'll say yes to is . . . [fill in that blank with power and purpose]."

Now breathe. There. You've done it. You've decided. Now you're safe to go into the conversation without having to play defense when you're not ready. You know your terms. Nice work!

Step 6: Decide What to Do If You Get a No

What will you do if you get a hard no? Ah, the almighty question.

If you get a no, even to your reserve, what are you going to do? Know the answer to that, and you'll never be blocked. The noes you get will be bumps in the road, not full-on roadblocks to your goals.

Ida, a woman who was underpaid and underappreciated, was ready to make an ask that would change it all. It was time for her to ask like an auctioneer. A house manager for a wealthy family, she was going to ask to triple her salary. And we had to ask the question, "If you get a hard no, even to your reserve, what will you do?" Confronted with this question, Ida realized that if she got a hard no, it would be time for her to find a new job, a new role, and a new family to work with. She had tears. Then she had clarity. And she resolved to pursue a salary and scope of role that reflected how she valued herself.

Your decision on what you'll do if you get a no can be as dramatic as Ida's, or it can be smaller and incremental. When we were kids, if we asked Mom for a candy bar, and she said no, what'd we do? Ask Dad. Or ask Grandma or Auntie. We'd hit a no, but there was usually a next step that still gave us another avenue.

If you get a no, you have options. Think, *I'll*:

- *escalate via my next skip-level meeting.*
- *move to part-time work and start consulting.*
- *pitch to the second most reputable program.*
- *self-publish.*

- *double down on the commercial portion of my real estate business.*
- *move departments.*
- *host an event with the other nonprofit I like.*

Now you can see beyond the no.

Take a look at your goal, your move, your ask, and your reserve and answer the following prompt:

"If I get a no, even to my reserve, I will [fill in the blank] _____
_____ as my next step."

Now, look at it. Look at your next step. Notice how you feel. Notice what thoughts may be floating by. Does articulating your next step have some lightness to it? Does it feel empowering to your ask? Does it give you a sense of groundedness? Are you saying to yourself, *Holy shit. Yes, that's what I'm gonna do?*

My hope for you is that it anchors you. Even if your decision has sadness in it, like it did with Ida, my hope is that it lets you know you have options. That you understand that you own your path. The big ask you make is an important moment, and there is life beyond the no. Your life and your goals do not belong to an answer you get from someone else. They belong to you.

Your Ask Plan

Great! You did it! Those six steps will help you identify a powerful ask whenever you have a a situation and goal that could use one. Now it's time to lay it all out and put a timeline on it. Use the prompts below to complete your Most Powerful Ask Plan. Notice the prompts start with the ask and work through your reserve, include your next step plan if you get a hard no, and feature a prompt you can use over and over: "What does it mean for me to make radical asks?"

Take a few minutes now to fill in the prompts below.

What: I am asking for _____.

Who: I am asking [person/organization] _____.

Minimum: My reserve is _____.

When: I will ask on _____.

Alternative: If I get a hard no, I will _____.

Inquiry: What does it mean for me to make radical asks?

Your answers to that last question will change over time. Today, it may mean challenging your assumptions or taking a risk. Tomorrow, making radical asks may mean delighting in standing up for your dream. Another day, it might mean forward movement or a recognition that a restart might be the result and that it's worth it to you to find out what happens when you ask. This inquiry at the end of your ask plan lets you circle back to your relationship with asking so you can stand in the power of asking big.

Keep reflecting on this inquiry. Ask yourself this question as you craft each ask you make, starting today. Notice how your answer changes over time. When you check in with yourself as you go, you may find that asking big transforms from something you dread doing to something that fills you with delight.

Find a digital download of the Most Powerful Ask Plan at asklikean auctioneer.com

---

IT'S JOURNAL TIME! (Not the journaling type? Then just reflect while you're organizing your junk drawer, sitting in the sun, dusting the baseboards, or downward dog-ing on the yoga mat you forgot you had and just found.)

You just built a very nice Most Powerful Ask Plan. Take a look at it and answer the following questions:

- How do you feel?
- Where do you feel it?
- What do you notice about your Most Powerful Ask Plan?
- What do you make of that?

CHAPTER 19

Storytelling and the HOW to Say It

C ongratulations! You've made your totally awesome and rock solid Ask Plan. You're so clear on your goal and the big move you need to make that gets you closer to your goal. You know your ask, it's a ZOFO ask, and you know you may get a no—and that if you do, you'll increment down until you find what works for the both of you. And if you get an instant yes, you'll know you may have left something on the table, but you'll be OK with it because it's way above what you would have asked if you were just aiming for a yes in the first place. You're all prepped with a plan for what you'll do even if you get a no across the board. You've adopted a disposition of openness and generosity while holding your boundaries and leaning on your reserve to let you know what a no is for you. You can totally see that there is an offer inside your ask so you can approach your asking moment knowing that this ask you are about to make is good for everyone—and that makes you feel great. You're reminding yourself that you are an agent for your purpose and that ties this exciting moment to something worth taking a risk for.

You have a plan. But now you're having that weird realization that you need the words. There's this feeling of *I've got it! But how do I actually ask for it?!*

You've got the *what*. Now it's time for the *how*.

It's time for some storytelling frameworks to help you put together the set up and the ask. Whether you're writing an email, sitting in a one-on-one with your manager, in a conference room, or on a video call, you gotta get your story straight so you can land that ask in a way that gives it the absolute best chance of doing for you what it's meant to do.

The storytelling approach and moves below are designed to help you put together a script for yourself. While we are asking like an auctioneer and aiming for a particular number or thing we think will threaten a no, I want to help you set it up with a story that does three important things: (1) makes it possible for you to make the ask clearly and confidently, (2) gives that big ask the best chance of getting a yes that is as close to the no as possible (remember the ZOFO), and (3) helps you ask by exercising empathy, as empathy gets good results.

STORYTELLING IS AN EDITING JOB

Some people think that storytelling is something bigger than it actually is or needs to be. Like it's some art form reserved for only the creative elites. For folks with a talent and a certain swagger or mysterious genius. It conjures images of sitting around a fire being transfixed by the most charismatic, vest-wearing outdoorsman in the world. Or the bespectacled, pipe-smoking beatnik. It begs you to imagine the gestalt that is the Silicon Valley pitch culture with its metaverse-y SaaS tech giants and self-driving whiz kids pitching the next reality to a room of serious-looking investors in designer glasses. It makes you think *Hamilton* and Steve Jobs and sophisticated ad agencies. Stand-up comedians and Brené Brown. How can we compete with these storytellers?

The truth is, anyone can tell a story. You don't have to be a master wordsmith or have a distinctive voice like Maya Angelou. You don't have to be anything but you.

You just need to put together some ideas in a certain order based on some stuff you already know.

You don't have to start with the overwhelm of a blank page. You're not creating something out of nothing. We're going to gather some information, arrange it in a certain order based on your goals, and edit it up. It's an editing job.

Don't be fancy. You don't need to be clever and catchy. You don't need to figure out how to make your ask not sound like an ask. You can make your ask a great story by putting it into context, helping it roll off your tongue or your keyboard. It will take

> *"Putting your story together is an editing job—take the information you have and make it work for you."*

some thought and some planning, but it doesn't have to be some work of art—it just needs to do the job.

Putting your story together is an editing job—take the information you have and make it work for you. We're going to gather the information we have—about who you're asking, about what you're asking for and why, and about what matters to you and to the person you're asking—and arrange it in a way that forms a compelling story.

Our approach will be simple:

First, you're going to gather some information.

Then, you're going to choose a framework. (I'll provide them, and you can mix and match.)

Last? You'll build a story using the information you've gathered and the framework you choose. (Boom!) Let's get going.

Step 1: Identify and Name a Topic

When I step on stage as an auctioneer, I don't start with "I'm going to ask you for money." No. We're not talking about that yet. When I write my script, I'm asking myself what I want to talk about during my two-minute set up before the auction starts and the asking gets going based on the context of the situation. Am I talking about the power of collective giving? Am I talking about the importance of early education? Am I talking about a legacy of contribution from the executive director? Am I talking about fun?

You have a topic too. And the topic is not just *my ask*. It's the topic that's relevant to the context of and for your ask.

Imagine you're about to have a discussion with your manager, to begin a topic that is a container for what you're about to ask. Maybe the topic is *my development plan* or the *performance review*, but maybe it's bigger and something like, *the team's collaboration* or *struggles in moving to agile* or *revenue*.

You're not gonna start the conversation with "I'm here to talk about my shitty compensation package and to ask for a boatload more money."

No. The topic isn't what you're going to do—your topic is the thing you want to discuss that *positions* what you're going to do.

So maybe for the above shitty compensation scenario, you want to identify and name the topic "The future of the business."

Stuck? Ask yourself: *What am I* really *talking about here?* This is an information gathering activity, not a creative act. So just look at the field of topics that your ask could belong to and pick the one that makes the most sense to you.

Remember, you get to choose! The right one is the one you select because it makes sense, works for you, and feels, sounds, or looks right.

The topic you choose creates the positioning for the discussion you're about to have, the ideas you'll share, the ask you'll make, and the outcomes you're intending to create. So get clear on that first. Write it down.

Step 2: Craft Your Ask

You've already created your Ask Plan, so just grab the ask part and write it down whenever you're sketching out the information you're gathering for your story fodder.

So now you have a topic and an ask. Great. You know what you wanna talk about and what you're gonna ask for. You have positioning in the form of a topic, and action in the form of an ask.

These are the anchors for your story.

But we don't have enough information yet to start putting content together into a story. We need to do a little more reconnaissance that will help guide us.

Step 3: Take Inventory of Their Questions

The person you're making your ask to is gonna have questions. Consider what they might possibly be now to inform how you might address them through the content of your story. Take a few minutes and consider what questions you think they'll have, even if they may not ask them directly.

If this is a new relationship (I do a lot of these types of calls to advance my own business), you may anticipate that one of their questions might be: "Who the hell are you and can I trust you?" If you're talking to your manager or a board member or a peer, you may have a better sense of more granular questions they might need to have answers to over the course of your discussion or pitch.

Things like:

- What is this about?
- Where is this coming from?
- How is this tied to our strategic objectives now?
- What's in it for me?

Just take an inventory of possible questions. Later, we're going to use the list you make to keep your story on track so your audience gets their needs met. We've got to bring them along, not slam them with a demand.

Not sure what their questions might be? Do your best to anticipate what they *could* be. Or send them an email that says, "Next week we're meeting to talk about [fill in your topic]. Are there any specific questions you'd like me to make sure I answer?" Or ask a friend or colleague what questions they think you should be ready for. People love to gossip. Keep it positive, but asking others' thoughts on what questions your audience may have goes a *long* way for you as you plan your story.

Step 4: Take Inventory of Their Motivations

Your audience has a reason to say yes to you. It's time to gather some information about their motivations connected to your ask. If you know your audience, you can just take a beat and write down what you think will spark their desire to make your ask work. And these things can be super data driven or the feely-est of touchy feely.

You're not cracking some super specific twenty-six-digit code that if you get it wrong will cause the safe to blow. No. You're just taking some time to consider who these people are and what's important to them. These people who have their own needs and desires and egos and plans. Do some light internet stalking. Read some of what they've written. Know someone who knows them? Call and ask, "What are they like? What gets them excited?" You know, that kind of stuff. Have a conversation with yourself.

My audience is motivated by:

- Being seen as smart
- Being first in any market
- The values they espouse
- Having fun
- Feeling connected
- Helping others
- Advancing themselves and shining
- Scientific approaches
- Data insights
- The big picture
- The little picture
- Smart tactics
- Being a mentor
- A social cause

The list goes on. Don't let yourself get away with "I have no idea." That's bullshit. You *do* know. You know *something.* Or you can guess if you have to.

Gather what you do know and take a shot at anticipating their motivations. It'll help you put together your story.

Step 5: Take Inventory of Their Objections

So far, you've gathered up your topic name, ask, questions you think your audience will have, and some recognition of what motivates them. Now it's time to address the dark side. What do you think could be their objections to your ask?

Do they hate change?

Are they always worried about making the wrong decision?

Is considering your ask going to require they go sell your idea by making a request to other stakeholders, and they don't like that?

Do they not trust/know you enough?

See what we're doing here? We're uncovering their potential resistance points. I bet you can come up with an answer for how to address each of these. Even if your answer is "Yes, you'll need to sell it to the leadership team, Dan. I've prepped you some content you can use to explain why this project is so critical to the success of the product launch and why I'm the one to run it."

You've gathered your information, one way or another—assembled it into a list in a nice notebook, blasted it up on a whiteboard, or maybe even stuck sticky notes on your desk. Great. Now take a look at it and consider what all that information tells you. Does it tell you that the way to set up the ask is to focus on, for example:

- The business value and how easy saying yes will be for your audience
- The aspirational nature of what your audience cares about
- Avoiding pitfalls
- The financial upsides they care about
- Their desire to win and not lose

Based on the information you have, you can pick an approach, or positioning, that you think best fits your audience.

PICK YOUR MOVE

Let's talk about formulas. But before we do, let's talk about content blocks. Each story formula below is built of content blocks. Content blocks are exactly what they sound like—a block of content dedicated to a specific topic or idea. You can create and stack any kind of content blocks you want. Like, one content block to describe "the problem," one to describe "the solution," one to name and talk through "roadblocks and pitfalls," and another to talk about "next steps." Think of content blocks as a chapter in a . . . wait for it . . . story! In this case, we're gonna limit the content blocks to these five:

- Your mission/purpose (here's what I see is important to you and what you're trying to do or avoid doing)
- My mission/purpose (here's what I'm trying to do)
- My goal (here's one way I'm doing it)
- Also . . . (where those two intersect)
- The ask . . . (the thing I'm asking for and how much of it I'm asking for)

You can decide what to focus on and with how much detail to include in each content block. It could be a single sentence, a paragraph, or a full-on narrative for each. And you can, obviously, customize, title or not title each block, and add any new ones as needed if you don't like these. Either way, you know what you're addressing with each content block and you get to decide how you address it. We're going to consider the five blocks I mentioned and then use the below story approaches to remix them into what works for the specific audience you're talking to.

I don't watch pro wrestling. Like, at all. But I have taken and completed exactly one jiujitsu class as a guest. If you ask any kid or wrestling fan, or if you take a jiujitsu class, you'll hear about moves or techniques—throws, takedowns, joint locks, sweeps, and so on. In pro wrestling, you'll hear about the Powerslam or the Suplex. In jiujitsu, they have names for a sequence of positions strung together with a specific objective. And often the move you choose, as far as I can tell, has a lot to do with the strength, skill, size, and position of your opponent.

When we're making an ask, our audiences are not our opponents per se—they're our collaborators—but you get the drift. We're going to borrow from the world of professional wrestling (I can't believe I'm saying that) and build four storytelling approaches you can choose from to use with your audiences and then leverage content blocks to frame up your ask. This will help you take the inventories you made and put them into action. And like any great wrestler, you'll add your own style and flair.

Your story approach is like a wrestling move. And wrestling isn't a single action—it's a sequence of actions put together to make moves. That's how you're going to build your story.

Here goes: We're going to name each story approach like it's a wrestling move, but a little friendlier, and bent toward our own realities. Plus, I'll share some clues on when to use which move.

The Gut Cincher

The Gut Cincher is best for emotional audiences who are super vocal and clear about what they care about. These audiences, when found in the wild, are often retelling stories that touched them. Talking about people they admire and saying things like, "Oh my god, I just love that!" These audiences have a sense of wonder and curiosity and love a good rom-com. They light up when we talk about values, the meaning behind their work, and how any decision affects people. They want to make sure things are working for everyone, and they live a lot in their feelings. They have big feels.

In these cases, you'll want to appeal to their guts ASAP. The sequence of blocks here is:

- **Their mission/purpose.** Talk about their mission and purpose using a lot of feeling language. Appeal to what really matters to them, possibly citing examples where you've seen, read, or heard about things they've done or championed that had a real impact on the people around them or for a particular demographic. Talk about their mission using stuff that's moving. Don't pull punches. Get into the feels.

- **My mission/purpose.** As you describe your mission and purpose, place emph-A-sis on the right syll-A-ble, and make sure it's on the part that makes us well up. If you have the choice between citing a disembodied data point or using an actual story of someone you've come across in your mission-driven work, choose the personal story. You have lots of content choices here—go for the gut.
- **My goal.** Make it concrete, and nail the goal to the impact you're trying to have. Again . . . feeling language.
- **And so** . . . Here's where your two worlds come crashing together and how what your audience cares about and what you care about advances what they care about. This is the emotional crescendo and sets you up for a strong ask.
- **The ask** . . . Nail it with an ask that feels like a hug.

The above sequence of content blocks works great, and you can fill in the content for each in a way that appeals to this particular type of audience. Take a second and notice who, in your life or professional setting, could be a good fit for the Gut Cincher. I'll tell you who: me! I'm a sucker for a good Gut Cincher—it'll take me down every time. As we continue with the next three, start to think about who each strategy might be a good fit for. Just as a thought experiment, not a mandate. I simply want you to start to connect these tools to real-life people and real-life asking so you can get your real-life goals.

The Brain Teaser

The Brain Teaser is for audiences who love to be smart, get to the point, and describe themselves as technical or "data driven." "Show me the data!" they exclaim. They love models and schematics and plans. If it doesn't work on paper, it doesn't work. They want to know before they go. And they want to know you get the logic of any decision or recommendation. They want to know that you have good reasons for your choice to buy donuts instead of croissants—they are interested in the explanation that reverses the logic so they can rubber stamp it, green light it, or grapple with it. These audiences want to know how it all fits together. Lucky for you, these audiences appreciate the same block sequence as in the Gut Cincher, though the content within each block is more data focused—more . . . precise, shall we say. These folks live a lot in their heads. They have big thoughts.

In this case, you'll want to appeal to their minds ASAP. The sequence of blocks here is:

- **Their mission/purpose.** When you're selecting the *how*, you might talk about their mission and purpose, bust out your mechanical pencil, and get ready to be precise. As you acknowledge their mission and purpose, choose language and descriptions that appeal to the type of thinking brain that loves seeing the math work. They don't care how it feels to drive efficiencies in the organization; they care about the satisfaction that comes with optimizing by 2 percent—so use that in how you talk about them to them—how you reflect their mission or purpose back to them.

- **My mission/purpose.** This is not the time to talk about the mushy stuff. For example, in my communications work, I might talk about my mission to have every leader operate from the belief that their voice is a tool for alignment in the business . . . *because* that cuts down on the number of business cycles it takes to ship a product or feature. See what I did there? I could have framed my mission to have every leader operate from the knowledge that their voice is a tool for alignment in the business as something that helps cultivate a culture of belonging when we have clarity. But nope, I'll save that for use when I need a good Gut Cincher.

- **My goal.** Get concrete here with a brief, clear goal that tracks logically with your mission—keep it simple, dispassionate, and, for Chrissake, don't mist up. Now's not the time.

- **And so** . . . Logic, logic, logic! Now make the connection using the logic that works. Appeal to the brain. Help them put on their thinking caps and find the story in this section that gives them a little insight that makes them pull off their glasses, place one end of the earpiece between their teeth, turn down the corners of their mouth, and nod quietly with the visible intellectual prowess of a tenured math genius.

- **The ask** . . . Keep it matter-of-fact, Jack. This is a *brain* teaser after all—keep it neck up.

See a pattern? I'm offering each of these content blocks in the same sequence, but the content *inside* the blocks—what you talk about and how you talk about it—can change based on the move you're choosing. You can always just use these blocks in the same order I'm showing here. Some of us like a recipe that's simple, repeatable, and predictable—a formula that you know works every time. And some of us? We like to mix it up and add our own flair. And you can. How? By reordering the content blocks however you think works best. After we get through the next two moves, I'll show you an example of a remixed set of content blocks for one of these moves. So hang tight, and let's take a look at the next two strategies.

The Power Dunk

The Power Dunk is ideal for audiences who crave recognition. Who light up when their work and impact is seen. They love to know they've done well. They love to win and get a medal for it. They're champions, and they are unafraid of shining. So shine on them! They've got their own goals and ambitions, and those ambitions need to know they're being included in the equation real quick. You're gonna help these folks feel that everything you're asking for is tied to helping them look great, get what they need, grow their network, or level up. You better make sure you're extra, extra clear on what the offer is inside your ask, and you better deliver it on a silver platter when it's time. These folks live a lot in their goals. They have big goals.

In this case, you'll want to appeal to their ambition ASAP. The sequence of blocks here is:

- **Their mission/purpose.** Congratulations, recognition, and respect. That may be a good way to talk about what you see is important to this ask-ee. If you're using the Power Dunk, choose content that powers up your audience. Don't be over-the-top, but keep in mind that shining on these folks is a good thing, and make the way you talk about them reflect that.
- **My mission/purpose.** While folks who like a good Power Dunk like recognition, they often also like people like them. So here, feel free to shine a big light on what matters to you in a way that lets them know they're in good company and can shine as bright as they want.
- **My goal.** Make this feel like an aspirational, forward-focused goal that has a great chance of allowing them to be first, be big, and be awesome!
- **And so** . . . Make them look great by connecting what you're doing with what they care about. When they see that what you're doing has potential to make them look like a hero? That's a winning strategy.
- **The ask** . . . Don't be shy about being a little effusive here. Especially if you've set up your ask with a big, juicy, winner story, this ask can feel like a chance for us to go do something awesome together. Are you clear on the offer inside your ask? Drop it like it's hot.

Still the same content block sequence here, but the content inside can change. Who in your life or work or network is that super goal-oriented ambitious type (ahem, besides you) that you think the Power Dunk would be a great choice for? I use this one a lot in sales contexts, leading with the business goals of the stakeholder I'm talking to and helping them see how we can tie the business goals, their goals, and mine all into a tight little package. It's a goal fest. A goal party. Goooooooaaaaaaalllllllll!

The Catapult

One of my faves, the Catapult is an oldie but goodie move that's great for the audiences who are always mission driven. They love and lust over having a mission, hearing about others' missions, and staying on mission. They love huge impacts, big ideas, and grand challenges with a strong dose of social impact mixed in. They're concerned with making change where change needs to be made. Do they see themselves as activists? Not always—but they are definitely here for it. They love to get to the *why* of it all, and they need to see the bigger picture. At dinner, they won't shut up about that new piece of research or that new policy proposal. They are not academics necessarily, but are academia adjacent. They are intellectuals and businesspeople who are committed to making an ever-greater impact. These folks live a lot in their higher purpose. They have big purpose.

In this case, you'll want to appeal to their sense of purpose ASAP. The sequence of blocks here is:

- **Their mission/purpose.** With a bit of a more sober tone, the Catapult is the intellectual's version of the Gut Cincher, so choose content to describe what's important to your audience that uses big statements backed up by empirical, qualitative, quantitative, grounded theory research or latest life hack that's caught fire socially. The Catapult is a great way to draw on current and future focused ideas that you know your audience is involved with, champions, or respects.

- **My mission/purpose.** The more avant-garde you can be, the better. Tell the truth, be authentic and real, but if you have a choice, choose the big idea language and examples.

- **My goal.** Whoa. Make this matter. Position your goal as noble and realistic but also as a stretch as these audiences love a BHAG—Big Hairy Audacious Goal. They're not afraid of going to the moon and they're OK with goals that may fail because it's the spirit of the thing that matters, and failure is just a learning tool!

- **And so** . . . Boom! Blow their minds with how what you're doing will help them bring to life what they care about. And give them something to brag about when they sponsor you.

- **The ask** . . . Is there an offer inside this ask? Absolutely, but it may not be directed at them. It may be a bank shot. Meaning they say yes to you and someone/something they care about gets something material. A nonprofit; a mentee they are, well, mentoring; a movement they support. And make the ask part very matter-of-fact and sober—but also the kind that makes us lean in. It's secret dealings to advance a big idea, a big mission, and a big future.

The Catapult can be so fun and exciting to speak to. It is future- and impact-focused, filled with aspiration and inspiration and action. It takes the greater good into account and lets you exercise those purpose muscles in a way that can bolster your storytelling for the better. One pro tip: It doesn't work if you don't go all the way. It's hard to be compelling when you're just slightly highlighting their purpose. In this case, you gotta *go* there and use the language they use when talking about purpose so it is clear, identifiable, and familiar.

LET'S DO THE MIX UP

Earlier, I said that if you like to go your own way, you can remix—or what my kids call "Do the Mix Up"—with these content blocks. They work in the sequence I've shared above, but if you want flexibility? Go for it!

Mix and match each content block into a different order based on what you think will work best for your audience. I often write mine up or outline them in the order I've presented above and then ask myself two questions:

- Does this order create the strongest effect?
- If I Did the Mix Up, how would I reorder the content blocks for the biggest impact?

For example, if I were using the Gut Cincher, maybe I'd Do the Mix Up like this: I'd start with **the ask** for maximum drama and then dip into talking about **my mission/purpose** and paint a really nice emotional picture about it. I could then talk about **the goal** to offer the reason for the ask, all the while appealing to the feelings this goal evokes. Then I could speak to how what

Ask Like an Auctioneer

matters to me touches what's important to you and **your mission/purpose** in a way that taps into all the feels, and then wrap it all up with a nice, juicy **and so** that makes it clear how what I'm doing helps you do what matters to you—and then invite your response. See? You can Do the Mix Up.

But Doing the Mix Up doesn't end here. The best wrestlers have their own unique styles. They've made their moves their own. I've shared with you four basics, but you can take them, remix them, and add your own flair to make new moves that are uniquely yours. I'd love to hear what you come up with. Maybe you'll make a move called the Green Banana or the Silky Whale or the Minivan Muscle Drop. Name them and claim them, and start to notice what they do for you and how you'll use the content blocks to bring your asks to life. Start to notice how they support you no longer holding your breath—how they help you take action, ask for more, and, over time, get it.

IT'S JOURNAL TIME! (Not the journaling type? Then just reflect while you're bored, eating lunch by yourself, vacuuming your car, or waiting for the train.)

This journal activity is something to help you connect this chapter to your real world. If you can make the connection below, you can do it anywhere, anytime.

Pick three people in your life and list them below.

Which of the four storytelling moves match with each person? The Gut Cincher, the Brain Teaser, the Power Dunk, or the Catapult. Why?

1. Name _____
   Best-fitting move _____
   Because _____.
2. Name _____
   Best-fitting move _____
   Because _____.

194

3. Name _____

   Best-fitting move _____

   Because _____.

Now, turn it on yourself: Which storytelling move should someone use on you? Why?

Use the move _____.

Great! Now go try one of these moves, and trust you'll get better at this as you practice.

CHAPTER 20

. . . And Other Things Women Freak Out About

In keynotes and workshops where I teach the principles you're reading about in this book, I hear a lot of the same questions and concerns. I'm sharing the ones I hear most often in this chapter, since they might be questions you're having right about now. Here, I'll answer them the best I can so you can worry less and ask for more.

"Yeah, but if I want to ask for THAT, how do I know I'm not delusional?"
I know it can feel a little out-of-body to make asks that seem out of reach even if they're honestly *the* thing that will get you the resources you need for the goal you have for yourself *and* you can back your shit up with evidence, examples, social proof, or whatever you need to make your ask connect with your audience. But don't let that *whoa!* feeling allow you to talk yourself into thinking you're crazy. Women ask me, "How do I know this ask isn't just delusional?"

Because it's not delusional. I already know that. But if you need a way to check yourself—to know that the ask is just big and weird or challenges an expectation that you or someone you're asking might have—you can use this: If you can explain it, you can ask for it.

Even if your explanation is, "Those are my rates" or "It's time," or "This is what I'm looking for to reach my goal," or "Because I want to."

If you can explain it, you can ask for it.

"What If I ask and it kills the negotiation?"
If your initial ask is a disqualifying event, then the person you are asking is likely not the right partner, mentor, client, or boss for you. And that's OK. Move on because, remember, your market is bigger than the room and you want partners—on your journey to your goals—who will be in conversation with you and who will try to find that equilibrium between what you want and what they'll say yes to.

> " *If you can explain it, you can ask for it.* "

If you get an initial no, follow up. Ask questions, seek to understand, and signal that you're up for a discussion. But do it while holding onto your reserve like a seven-figure winning lottery ticket you just found in your jeans pocket from a week ago, right before they went through the wash.

"How do I make the ask so I don't look greedy/overly ambitious/pushy?
Ladies, we've spent too long twisting ourselves into pretzels in our attempts to control how we're perceived. I'm not going to help you do that. If we spend all our time trying to figure out how not to be, we have no time or energy or spirit left over to figure out how *to* be who we actually are.

Instead, here are some better questions you can use as prompts in your preparation for the asks you'll make.

- "How might I make it clear that my ambitions are going to benefit what matters to my ask-ee?"
- "How might I stay strong in my conviction even in the face of criticism about my ask?"
- "How might I own my ambition as a positive attribute?"

"I've made the ask. How do I get someone off the fence?"

See chapter eight. Also, take the silence you get after an ask as a no. Then, move on. Not getting silence but instead getting breadcrumbed? (You know, those stalling techniques your manager or client or potential client uses, like "later," "not now," or "next quarter . . .") Take the breadcrumbing as a no. They haven't said "yes" and they haven't said "no," and keeping you on the hook without advancing your agenda is a waste of your time. Set a deadline for an answer, communicate that deadline, and see if they're in or if they're out. Oh, and have a plan for what you'll do in the face of either answer so you know what's next no matter what they say.

"My goals are kind of a secret. I'm shy about saying them out loud. Is that a problem?"

Oh man, nobody can help you if they don't know what your goals are! You can and should talk about what you're working toward with everybody and anybody who you suspect is going to listen openly. Why? Because it's the story! And it's the thing that other people will help you with when you ask for what you need to support your pursuit.

There are two unintended bonuses for talking about your goal(s). One is that you get practice. Lots of it. You get practice honing your *Here's What I'm Up To*, narrowing it down so that it becomes spicier, more succinct, and more specific. When you talk about your goal(s), you can take note of what resonates with your listen-

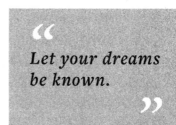

> **Let your dreams be known.**

ers and what piques their curiosity, and it can expand your thinking about how to talk about your goals when you use them to set up an ask. It's pitch practice! The second bonus is that people will have unexpected connections, offers, and ideas to help you get what you need to reach that goal. "Oh, you want that? Have you talked to Beth in design? They're looking for someone to do exactly that!" See? Let your dreams be known. Helping the world understand the context of the asks you make can help your ask-ee see why they're so big, bold, or new. Build context for better results.

"I just feel so freaked out. I just can't. I stop myself from asking all the time."
Here's where to start: Fall in love with your goals. Talk to them like they're precious little gifts. Love them like you love your little niece or nephew who you desperately want to see grow into their full potential. Build them up. Give them a pep talk. Let them know you are rooting for them. Fall so in love with your goals that your love for them is greater than your fear of rejection.

> " *Fall so in love with your goals that your love for them is greater than your fear of rejection.* "

You treat goals this way all the time for other people; do it for yourself and for your trembling little ask, knowing it is actually a badass strategy just waiting to reach its potential.

Think about all the times you've told your nephew that "it's going to be OK! You're wearing a life jacket, and it's just like that time you jumped off the dock at the lake. It's just a little higher!!! I believe in you, buddy, and I'm right here cheering you on. You got this!"

And then he jumps and maybe belly flops a bit and scares the shit out of himself—but then he's like, "Auntie! That stung but I'm gonna do it again cuz it was fun!"

Like that. Give yourself, and your ask, a little pep talk.

That love-fest around your goal may just activate your tiny genius and get it cheering right with you and working its magic in the way only it can.

What if the ask I make doesn't do what it was supposed to do?
See chapter sixteen—it's a good one. Unintended outcomes are all part of the messy learning process as we stumble toward our goals. There will be surprises, big and small, good and bad, and everything in between. The thing is: None of this is fixed! You get to ask, learn, and iterate. You get to experiment

and try new things. I just don't want you to leave money and opportunity on the table while you do the asking, learning, iterating, and experimenting. I've asked for plenty of things that I thought were the silver bullets to reaching my goals and, nope . . . didn't work out that way. But asking was never a waste because along the way more folks learned about my goals and I learned more about what matters to me and to others. You gotta get in the mess, because this process is messy and alive and wonderful. Get off your own back about everything fitting together like a complete Lego set. It won't. There will be leftover pieces and parts you can't quite figure out. But it's better than sitting around here all day and waiting for something to happen.

"What do I do when I get a yes but it never goes anywhere?"
This is breadcrumbing. You're getting breadcrumbed.

If you've made an ask—let's say to take on a certain type of project or to become a people manager or maybe move your pay structure to include a bonus—but months, quarters, maybe even full freaking calendar years have gone by and you've seen zero movement to action, then that yes is an unfulfilled promise. It's just sitting there like a big old PAC-MAN machine with no power. You have it, but you don't *really* have it.

Let's look back at chapter eight (the one where you learned to ask people if they were in or out). When I'm standing in front of an audience conducting an auction, I use the phrase "Are you in, or are you out?" to wrap this damn thing up quicker by forcing my audience to tell me right where they stand. Sometimes they're in or out, and sometimes they're breadcrumbing me, looking indecisive, or stalling. In this case, I get to decide what to do. I take their silence as a no. And you can too.

When you're told yes, but nothing happens and you're met with *next quarter, next performance review, next time, or the next time after that,* or just plain silence? Take it as a no. Why? Because you ain't got time.

And you can then flip to chapter ten's advice—remember that there are other people to ask, other scenarios where you can find what you need. Because it's true that you *will* get a no. Sometimes it's a no that will never turn into a yes. Sometimes it's a yes that's actually a no coated in breadcrumbs.

Either way, *you* get to decide how you want to take it and move on to find the market that is interested in the goods you're selling.

While you may ask for more and not get it this time, you will ask for more and get it over time so long as you continue moving forward.

"I know what I want to ask for, now how do I actually ask for it?"
In chapter nineteen you learned some storytelling tools—use them as needed. You *will* find a way to say it. What you need to do is recognize that you're not gonna break a deal because you said this word or that one. You want to come across as firm and empathetic, and you want to recognize that, in your ask, you are offering something. Beyond that, you can't spend forty-seven years wordsmithing what you'll actually say. There's a point where you're gonna have to rip that Band-Aid off and push send or just say it already. Do your best, and jump right into the deep end.

What if my ask makes them uncomfortable?
That's OK. Let them be uncomfortable. They can handle it. Lora, a badass winery owner, had to negotiate with a couple who wanted to host their wedding at her venue. In the negotiation, she told me she spent so much energy and time making sure they felt cozy about the boundary she'd put down when she got pushed to her reserve that it was as if setting down the minimum she'd be willing to accept and the minimum the business could afford was some personal affront to the buyers. "No. I'm not doin' that any more.

> **"**
> *While you may ask for more and not get it this time, you will ask for more and get it over time so long as you continue moving forward.*
> **"**

They're grown ass adults. They can handle a little tension, a little pressure. It's not my job to smooth over their feelings about my boundary. I can just say what it is, and, with a smile or not and, ask if they're in or if they're out."

That's right, Lora! They're grown ass adults. And actually, that tension is powerful. To say where you stand, kindly and honestly, and then stand in that tension is a superhuman and powerful move. The people you will negotiate with have feelings. Let them have them. They're OK. You have boundaries. Let yourself have them. You're OK.

It seems everyone in my family and friend circle has me on speed-dial and wants a piece of me. If I help them all for free, I'll never get to my actual clients. How do I set my pricing for friends and family? So tricky!

Some of you run small businesses, consulting practices, or coaching firms, and you are often the tree everyone barks up for a "friends and family" discount—or, worse, they just assume your wedding planning services, business coaching, accounting consultation, or whatever it is you charge folks for,

> **"**
> *You're not gonna break a deal because you said this word or that one.*
> **"**

is theirs for the taking. I get it, you want to understand how to price your services for friends and family so you don't get or feel taken advantage of. Because there's only so many hours in the day, and dollar bills matter for every one of those hours or products you work on. You don't need new pricing. You need a policy.

You already have your pricing—it's what you charge your clients right now. It's time now to create your friends and family *policy* so you don't have to reinvent the wheel and renegotiate your rate with yourself every time you confront a friends and family request.

Here's are some examples of what I mean:

- My policy is that the business can afford to give two hours, max, of wedding planning consultation to friends and family. After that, it's a contract with a specific scope of work for the business. For your closest friends and family (think: first connection like sister, brother, best friend; after that, I don't know you), I do a 10 percent discount on each project just like I usually would for clients.

- We don't do pro bono work for friends and family. It's our policy.
- I do one pro bono engagement per quarter, which is capped at a value of $5,000. I've already offered that slot to Cousin Marty, but I could do it for you next quarter. Would that work for you? No? Aww. So sad.

You can take it to the next level by creating and publishing your friends and family policy on a beautifully designed and shareable PDF you distribute at the next family dinner, reunion, or baptism. Or, as an unlisted webpage on your site, complete with a booking link you share specifically with friends and family for them to book a time to "discuss their options."

You have pricing. Get a policy.

What if I change my mind?

You can change your mind. Nora did. She's a researcher in a field where salary bands and grant budgets are tight and not very flexible. Nora was offered a research position in academia. She was so excited about the opportunity, and she accepted. Twenty-four hours later, she received the official offer and did a double check on the math, and . . . no. She wasn't having it. It was below her reserve and she needed to correct the situation. With kindness and honesty, she reopened the negotiation and asked for what she needed to make it work and *re*-sealed the deal. She was ready to have to say no if they had to say no. But instead, when she said, "No, but how about this?" they said, "Yes." It can't work out every time, but it can work out sometimes. You get to change your mind. And you get to ask for more and find out if they're in or if they're out.

IT'S JOURNAL TIME! (Not the journaling type? Then just reflect while you're doing the dishes, taking a hike, sitting on a park bench, or practicing spinning a pencil between your fingers in a perfect helicopter motion.)

Pause a moment to take inventory of where you're at by answering the following questions:

- When you think about asking big, what freaks you out?
- Which idea and strategy from part two's nine ideas can you use as strategies to empower your ask and would help you freak out less?
- Pick one or two, and write about what about them works for you.

CONCLUSION

You Can Ask for More and Get It When You Ask Like an Auctioneer

For the last week I've been walking around the house and the grocery store and my kids' sports practice and the orthodontist waiting room trying to figure out how to say goodbye to you. The moment has arrived.

I want to stay here with you all day talking about your dreams and goals and what you're building. I could listen for ages to the challenges you face and the big moves you need to make to get you one small but meaningful or enormous and thrilling step toward your goal. I could brainstorm all night about the asks you could make and the people you could make them of. I could hold your hand while you share with me what would make that ask a ZOFO one—it never gets old, listening to you scare yourself alive naming and claiming your ZOFO. I could use up all the space on the table to jot down notes while you tell me where your boundaries lie and watch your eyes light up when you tell me what your reserve is. I could pound that table when you plan what you'll do when you get a no even to your reserve.

I could stand beside you, waiting in the wings, while you step onto your imaginary stage, holding your mic with one hand and raising the other to command the room as you take a breath and ask like an auctioneer.

But instead, I'll just give you a lightweight Gut Cincher and say: I see you striving. Tipping your body into the wind and putting one foot in front of another with the promise of funding your startup, building something great, leading teams and movements, amplifying your economic viability, living the adventure you desire, and fulfilling your purpose at the end of your trek. I hear you grappling with what's next and finding the path forward that makes the most sense to you even as that logic requires some faith to make it from where you are now to where you are going.

With this book, these ideas, and my heart in my fist, I am taking a stab at the possibility that what I learned in a surprising hobby I picked up in my forties, paired with some good fun and great stories from women just like you, can put more money and decision-making power in your hands and change everything for all of us. And I'm trying to share these stories and make this difference in a way that feels like an adventure—full of joy and fun and celebration and heartbreak. This mission is grand, but we can pursue it, one ask at a time, and have a blast doing it.

Project: Ask Like an Auctioneer started as an experiment. It has helped many women ask for more and get it.

Teresa renegotiated her status with her employer so she could start a new career. She asked for more money for less time and got it. She asked bigger than she ever had before, and now she knows she can ask for more and get it when she asks like an auctioneer.

Deanna got honest with her manager and asked to change paths from sales to design. She pursued her dream, and they retained her talent! She was sure they'd say no. But she asked like an auctioneer and got a yes.

Tara put a number on a salary requirement that nearly turned her inside out. She was in her ZOFO and sent the number anyway, sure her ask threatened a no. She was tired of being a lawyer who was barely making it financially, and it was time to level up. After a tense few days of waiting for their response, she got the salary she was asking for, and her life changed forever. Now, Tara asks like an auctioneer whenever there's an ask to be made.

Macie accelerated her team's progress with one clarifying question, "Are you in, or are you out?" Her team had already said yes, but wasn't actually acting. She was tired of being breadcrumbed, so she stepped into her auctioneer persona and got the project unstuck.

Char asked to *own* the event strategy for her marketing team. She didn't just ask to work on a part of it, she asked to own the whole. damn. thing. Did she think she'd get a no? Yep. Did she willingly take the risk? Yep. Did she get what she asked for? Yep. She stepped into her ZOFO, asked for more, and got it.

But we're not stopping here. We're not stopping with the stories that we've accumulated so far. There are more of you. My goal is to help one million of you ask for more and get it, one ask at a time.

You are striving. Resourcing your dream for yourself. So use the ideas and strategies in this book starting today. I hope, deeply, that what I've shared here can be one ingredient in your journey that propels you toward your goals and helps you fulfill your purpose.

I hope, deeply, that you'll share these ideas and strategies. That you'll take the time to teach the women around you so asking in our ZOFO isn't the exception but the rule when it matters most. So that the ZOFO is our shared shorthand for celebrating each other's stretch and supporting each other's asks.

It's true that not all asks merit the auctioneer treatment, but the ones that matter—the ones that can resource your dreams and get you where you want to go faster—will always require you to ask like an auctioneer.

And, yes, you will be too much for some people. Those are not your people.

Recap and Resources

Resources available for download at www.asklikeanauctioneer.com.

How to Ask Like an Auctioneer

Ask Like an Auctioneer means:

- Aim for a no, and negotiate to a yes from there.
- Step into your ZOFO, because that's where the greatest potential is.

Empower your ask with these ideas from auctioneering:

People Are Irrational
- **Idea:** People are irrational, or *their* rationale is not *your* rationale.
- **Strategy:** Don't decide for your audience what they'll say "yes" and "no" to. Let them decide.

Know Your Reserve
- **Idea:** Know your reserve.
- **Strategy:** Always identify the minimum you'll accept so *you* know exactly what *you'll* say "yes" and "no" to.

Increments matter

- **Idea:** Increments matter.
- **Strategy:** Don't just split the difference on the dollars. Plan your increments and know what increments you have to plan.

Are You In, or Are You Out?

- **Idea:** Are you in, or are you out?
- **Strategy:** Make people decide so you know where you stand and can move on.

Price Is a Measure of Value, Not Your Worth

- **Idea:** Price is a measure of value, not of absolute worth.
- **Strategy:** Read the response you get to an ask as a measure of how the person you are asking values something, not as a measure of its absolute worth. Do this as a way to depersonalize the asks you make and the noes you get.

Your Market Is Bigger Than the Room

- **Idea:** Your market is bigger than the room.
- **Strategy:** Keep an abundance mindset to allow you to risk getting a no, knowing that there are other markets for your ask.

Purpose Drives Courage

- **Idea:** Purpose is a source of courage.
- **Strategy:** Get clear on your purpose, and use that to fuel your courageous asks.

Be an Agent for Your Purpose

- **Idea:** Be an agent for your purpose.
- **Strategy:** Act on behalf of your purpose in order to advocate for it with more freedom and less fear.

Inside Every Ask Is an Offer

- **Idea:** Every ask is an offer.
- **Strategy:** Find that offer to sell your ask for the highest bid.

RESOURCES

Build Your Ask Plan

The Goal: What's my goal? (Write a few sentences on what you dream about for yourself.)

The Move: What's *one* concrete step you can take that moves you closer to your goal?

The Ask: What is your ask?

The ZOFO: Is that ask big enough? What is the scary version of that ask?

The Reserve: What is the minimum counteroffer you'll settle for?

The next step: What will you do if you get a no?

Your Ask Plan

What: I am asking for _____.

Who: I am asking _____ (person/organization).

Minimum: My reserve is _____.

When: I will ask on _____.

Alternative: If I get a hard no, I will _____.

Inquiry: What does it mean for me to make radical asks?

Goal Categories and Goal Types

Goal categories

- Money
- Influence

- Authority
- Balance

Goal types

- Recognition
- Experiential
- Mastery

Storytelling Framework for How You Ask

Gather information as fodder for your story.

The Topic: Name the topic you'll be discussing to set up your ask.

The Ask: Write down how you'll make the ask in very specific and direct language.

Inventory Their Questions: What questions do you think they'll have about your topic?

Inventory Their Motivations: What would motivate them to say yes to your biggest ask?

Inventory Their Objections: What would stop them from saying yes to your biggest ask?

Pick a Storytelling Move to Set Up Your Ask

- **The Gut Cincher:** Best for emotional audiences who are super vocal and clear on what they care about.

  In this case, you'll want to appeal to their gut ASAP.

- **The Brain Teaser:** The Brain Teaser is for audiences who love to be smart, to get to the point, and to describe themselves as being technical or "data driven."

  In this case, you'll want to appeal to their mind ASAP.

- **The Power Dunk:** This move is ideal for audiences who crave recognition—who light up when their work and impact is seen. They love to know they've done well.

In this case, you'll want to appeal to their ambition ASAP.

- **The Catapult:** One of my faves, this oldie but goodie move is great for the audiences who are always mission driven. They love and lust over having a mission, hearing about others' missions, and staying on mission.

In this case, you'll want to appeal to their sense of purpose ASAP.

Swipe Files and Scripts (Not an Exhaustive List)

Use them as written or as thought starters!

For Asking
- "I'm looking for [insert thing you're asking for]."
- "I'd like [insert thing you're asking for]."
- "My target is [insert thing you're asking for]."
- "My ask is [insert thing you're asking for]."
- "I'm asking for [insert thing you're asking for]."
- "For this? I'd be at [insert thing you're asking for]."
- "I need [insert thing you're asking for]."
- "I'd say yes to [insert thing you're asking for]."
- "My policy is that I'd take [insert thing you're asking for]."
- "I've decided on [insert thing you're asking for]."
- "My rate is [insert thing you're asking for]."
- "This will require [insert thing you're asking for]."

For Saying No
- "Thank you, but that's not something I can say yes to."
- "That won't work for me."
- "I can't say yes to that."
- "I can't afford to say yes to that."

- "Thank you for the offer. I'm very focused on [insert thing you're focused on] and this isn't what I need to reach my goal."
- "That won't work for what I'm trying to do here."
- "That's outside what's possible."
- "I can't do that."
- "No."
- "Thanks so much, but no."
- "That's not something I'd be open to."
- "That doesn't work for what I need."
- "That's not something I can accept."
- "Thank you so much, but that's not enough for me to say yes."

For Opening Up a Negotiation After You Get a No

- "I understand. What *can* you do?"
- "Thanks for considering it. I'm open to seeing what's possible for us."
- "OK. Where are you on this?"
- "Thanks! Help me understand what might work for you."
- "OK. Can you say a little bit more about what you're thinking might work?"
- "What can you afford?"
- "Let's negotiate."
- "Are you open to discussing? I am."
- "Got it. I'd really like to keep talking. I'd be open to finding something that works for us both."
- "Darn it! I was so excited about this. Let's keep talking."

For Understanding Where They Stand (In or Out?)

- "Are you in?"
- "Are you out? Haven't heard from you."
- "Shall I close out this conversation?"
- "Where do you stand on this? If I don't hear from you, I'll assume we've closed this out."
- "Is this still on the table?"

- "Where are you at on this?"
- "Is this still in play?"
- "Is this a closed issue for you?"
- "Are you still considering this?"
- "Are we still talking about this? Or is it closed?"

Acknowledgments

B ig ups, shout-outs, and gratitude for a batch of folks who've made this book possible. To every one of you who brought the keynotes and workshops associated with this project to your communities, companies, and associations: Thank you. This book would not be as real as it is without the opportunities it's had to develop in the open and be work-shopped with the women and people it is intended to impact.

And there are a few specific folks I'd like to recognize, folks who were the instigators, momentum-makers, and pit crew for this race. To M. J. Ryan who was first to say, "Now, *that's* a book!" when *Ask Like an Auctioneer* was a secret I held and just a weird little idea. To Arthur Leon Adams III, Arthur Vibert, and Paul Jaffe, who just kept saying "keep going" and "yes, I can help you with that." For, like, four years, they just stood by and nudged me forward. Seriously, it meant everything.

To Maia Bazjanac, who was my muse, cooked warm bowls on writing re-treats, and let me read stuff out loud to her whenever I wanted. Maia kept me honest and held me to my own voice and never let me chicken out. To my read-ers, Kathryn Adams and Kat Gordon, who gave their time and attention and en-thusiasm for this project along with feedback of champions. To the editorial and production team at BenBella—and especially to Katie Dickman, who just made this all feel like a breeze. To Kevin Anderson, who found this book a home.

To all of you, thank you.

Index

About the Author

Photo by Myleen Hollero

Dia Bondi is the secret weapon behind some of the world's most influential brands, leaders, and VC-backed founders. She is CEO and founder of Dia Bondi Communications, which helps high-performance professionals speak with power and purpose at crucial communications moments to amplify their impact and reach their goals faster.

Following her curiosity, Dia attended auctioneering school and has since translated the techniques she learned into a program, called "Ask Like an Auctioneer," that prepares women to ask for more and leave nothing on the table, which catalyzed her mission to put more money and decision-making power in the hands of women so we can change everything for all of us.

Dia believes that you are your most compelling and impactful when you lead with who you are.

She lives with her family in Northern California.